LOUD SECRETS

a memoir

Jackie Pelletier

"The business of life is the acquisition of memories."

Mr.Carson,
Downton Abbey

JULY 1955

Old man Muller unzips his fly and takes the hand of the blond-haired, blue-eyed five year old girl and places it inside. "You can squeeze it; it will feel good." He hands the girl a thin wooden dowel with a small American flag and says "This is our little secret; don't tell anyone."

That five year old girl found herself in that upstairs dark shed in the big brown and yellow two-story apartment building on the corner in the south side of the city a few more times because her Mom and the neighbor lady who owned and lived in that building would tell her to take a few groceries up to Mr. Muller. Blind obedience and "do what your elders tell you;" that was the expectation. It was taught by our parents, the Catholic church and the nuns we spent time with everyday. We learned it and lived it. Even a little five year old shaking her head "no" didn't matter. That little girl didn't want to take groceries to Mr. Muller but she did want to see her little friend Marilyn, one year older than she. Marilyn lived in an apartment on the front side, first floor, of that brown and yellow two-story apartment building on the south side of the city with her family. Marilyn's younger cousin, Tess, and her family lived on the first floor on the back side of that same brown and yellow building. There was no "Stranger Danger" back then but people did know about dirty old men.

The smell of old wood in that shadowy shed, stored winter woolens, the red, white and blue flag and the click of the torn screen door shutting were forever embedded in her mind. Two years later her family moved across the bridge to the east side of the city, away from that big brown and yellow two-story apartment building.

FAMILY

My Franco-American Catholic relation was huge. They had migrated from New Brunswick, the Province of Quebec and the tip of Northernmost Maine. There were only five in my immediate family. Mom, Dad, my older brother Dan and my older sister Lucy. I was the baby. We had enough aunts, uncles and cousins to make multiple baseball and football teams. Dad had nine siblings and Mom had fourteen. Acadian French was spoken in the family homes but as we children began attending schools in central and northern Maine, English took over. All devout Catholics, Mass every Sunday, holiday and holy days of obligation. Lent meant that we would be on our knees in the living room every night before supper reciting the rosary and we would be giving up chocolates, or some other thing that brought us pleasure. Easter was shiny patent leather shoes, frilly hats, creased pants, starched shirts and roast lamb.

Dad had his own painting and wallpapering business. He worked hard but it seemed like he and Mom were always struggling. We had whatever was needed and now and again there would be some extras. I remember him taking the three of us target practicing in the local sandpit as early Fall approached. It was time to get the two rifles sighted in and ready for the November deer hunts. Dan would go with Dad deer hunting; am not sure if he wanted to, but, being a good son, he would do what Dad asked. In my late teens I would be the one to go with Dad a few times. I liked being in the woods but the pint of gin tucked in Dad's black and red wool hunting jacket always made me sad.

Dad was a weekend alcoholic. Didn't touch a drink during the week, but come 4:00 p.m. Friday afternoon it would begin. Can't say I ever remember seeing Dad sit down and nurse a drink. He always stood in the same place by the kitchen sink, opened the cupboard on the lower right side, took out a bottle of gin, poured it in a shot glass, threw his head back and downed it. This was repeated Saturday and Sunday, only it began as early as mid morning. I loved my Dad but when he would get drunk I would want to be as far away from him as I could. He wasn't abusive to us. He did not raise his voice often. But his drinking made me anxious. The physical changes I could see in his eyes and body gestures were unsettling to me. When he was sober he could carry a tune as smoothly and softly as a slow lapping wave could carry a leaf. I have a memory of him holding me in his arms as he stood singing "Bless This House" in the hallway of our home in front of a framed picture embroidered with that song.

One event in particular continues to stand out. It was a cold Saturday afternoon in late fall, and winter was rapidly approaching. Dad had been working in the yard cutting back shrubs and preparing the yard for snow and had been shooting shots of gin with every trip into the house. I came in from playing mid afternoon and needed to take my shower because it was Saturday and we all had to be cleaned and shined for eight o'clock Sunday morning Mass. I was angry and sad that Dad was drunk. When I got out of the shower I noticed the bathroom window was fogged over. As I stood wrapped in a towel, I took my finger and printed "Dad=Drunk" on the window. I then took my hand and wiped it off. Dad finished his work and needed to take his shower. Little did I know that my printed words would magically reappear on that refogged bathroom window. I was sitting at the kitchen table coloring when Dad came into the kitchen. He stood at the kitchen sink, faced the round mirror that hung on the wall just above the faucet, poured himself a shot, looked into the mirror and said to me, "Someday you will know what we did for you." I never looked up but knew he was talking about the message I had left on the bathroom window. Dad was a man of few words and when he told you something, the conversation was over. That's the way it was. I never recall my Mom and Dad arguing. Mom would say little to cause them to. I seldom saw Mom ever take a drink until much later in her life.

Dad was the main cook in the house. With Mom working the dinner shift most nights at a local restaurant, it was Dad who put dinner on the table. Mom always managed to have some homemade cookies or bars of some kind to snack on when we got home from school. Dad was a good cook. His time spent putting meals together in a lumber camp and then time cooking in a diner prepared him well to feed five or twenty-five, even on short notice.

Trips to the gritty sandy Atlantic ocean beaches or to inland lakes on summer Sundays were always a treat. Of course there was the eight o'clock Mass but upon arrival home a quick change of clothes, assembling of the red metal dented picnic cooler, woven picnic basket, swimsuits and sweatshirts and we would be off for the day. Usually relatives would gather at the same destination and while I loved having our cousins to swim and play with the presence of aunts and uncles would always lead to drinking. Mom did not drive at that time so we were forced to stay by the water late into the day. Our energy had been spent. We had wind swept hair, salt soaked bodies and longed to be home but we waited for Dad to stir from his two or three hour nap so that he could drive.

One very frightening memory I have was when I was about fifteen. Dad and Mom decided to take Dan and I to Lincolnville for a seafood dinner. It was Sunday, about noon when we left the house. Dad was driving, Dan was in the passenger seat and Mom and I were in the back seat of the car. I knew Dad had been drinking some. We were on route 17 heading east; a two lane road when Dad pulled out to pass a car. We were in a no passing zone. I looked ahead and could see a car coming straight for us. Dad accelerated, I saw eighty five on the speedometer, grabbed Mom, pushed her down on the backseat, heard Dan yell "Dad" as Dad swerved back into the lane ahead of the car he had passed. No one said a word. Dad pulled over to the side of the road, looked at Dan and said "You drive." Mom leaned into me and said softly "I think he scared himself." Not another word was said about that near tragic event, ever.

It seemed to me that Mom was always at work. She worked at the Augusta House as the dining room and banquet manager. This large hotel was just steps away from the Capitol Building and Mom was valued as the "hostess with the mostess" by many of the legislators who would frequently dine there. Mom liked the clientele and knew how they wanted their steaks cooked and their highballs made. White starched tablecloths and napkins, sterling silver place settings and brass chandeliers hung majestically from cream colored metal ceilings. These were all a perk for Mom. She had come a long way from waiting tables at her brother's diner. She always worked long difficult hours and enjoyed the climate the hotel offered her. I actually remember around the age of four or five crying when Mom would begin to get ready to leave for work in the late afternoon. Mom was home most weekends unless there were some big events at the hotel that she had to be present for like weddings or bar mitzvah's. Through the years, I, along with Dan and Lucy would work at that hotel.

I adored my Mom and missed her being home at supper time and bedtime. I do recall some bedtime stories and loved her singing in the kitchen as she baked or canned or cooked. She was seldom idle. Memories of her thin veined hands doing the wash, hanging out clothes, pushing an iron over and over a damp towel to steam Dad's shirts. I would help Mom bring the laundry in from a winter clothesline. I felt the damp and smelled the cold of frozen sheets and towels that would later thaw hanging in the basement washroom. If she sat down at night she would be darning socks or sewing buttons. Our home felt warm and safe. I loved my Mom and Dad. I believed what they said and trusted what they did.

Our aunts, uncles and cousins would gather frequently, mostly on week-ends, particularly Sunday late afternoons. Our main meal would be at one o'clock and we were so happy to have Mom home with us for Sunday dinner. That joy ended when Dad would all but pass out at the table, head hanging in his plate. I would silently look at Mom and pray that she would do some-thing,anything, to get him away from the table.

Dan and Lucy said nothing but their eyes told me they were pleading Mom for the same thing. Eventually, she would help him get to his chair in the living room where he would sleep for a couple hours. Upon waking, he would walk to that same spot at the kitchen sink, open the cupboard on the top right side and pop a couple of Alka Seltzer tablets in a glass and proceed to throw his head back and guzzle it down. This routine was usually followed by him making a pot of soup that would sit on the back burner of our large electric stove. A few extra cups of liquid were added to the soup when relatives appeared. Saltine crackers, butter and some sweet treats would be placed on the kitchen table as all were welcomed.

Holidays brought more family gatherings at our home. Drinking would start early and go long. One Aunt seemed to show up more than most and was present for birthdays and assorted occasions. Ida was not married and had a daughter, Doreen, the same age as my brother Dan. Most of the time Aunt Ida was accompanied by her male friend Arnold. Ida was one of my Mom's younger sisters. She lived with her mother, my Grandmother, whom we called Mémère (Ma-May). Ida would get as loaded as Dad sometimes. Open flirting went on, even in front of Mom. I was young; it would make my insides feel like I had eaten too many green apples, but I said nothing. I just tried to stay out of the way. When I was little I would sleep over at my Mémère's on some weekends. My Grandfather had died years earlier; I never knew him. Mémère remarried and moved to Waterville about twenty five miles north of us. Aunt Ida and Doreen lived with Mémère so I would see Ida often but seldom see Doreen because she was in a Catholic boarding school in Biddeford Pool, Maine. Some of my aunts disliked the man Mémère married. In fact, I remember being on Mémère's porch with a few aunts and hearing one of them say "He's a dirty old man; keep the little girls away." Back then I did not know to what they were referring. They were only married a few years when he died.

Mémère spoke only French and I was speaking more English than French but we always managed to communicate with each other. Hugs from my Mémère were frequent. I oozed her love and would say to her in our Acadian dialect "mois lem tui, tui lem mois" (I love you, you love me) and we would laugh. Time spent with my Mémère provided wonderful childhood memories for me. She would watch The Edge of Night every weekday afternoon and that would immediately be followed by a supper of chicken stew or some other delicious treat that had been simmering on her old kerosene stove. She was a devout Catholic who attended daily Mass and said the rosary every night on her knees before bed. Mémère was always ready for a card game with Canasta being her favorite. She was competitive, a gracious winner as well as a gracious loser. A nickel and a few pennies would be put into my hand to walk to the corner store to get her a bottle of Moxie and two pieces of penny candy for me.

November 1959, five days before Thanksgiving, I was nine years old; my Mémère died from a heart event. She was in the hospital just a couple of days. Mom took me to see her. A few of my aunts and uncles were standing in the hospital hallway when we arrived. I remember how sad everyone looked. As I entered the room, I searched for the bed but all I could see was a big plastic tent attached to some machines. That was the first time I had seen an oxygen tent but it would not be the last. The dull slate blue walls appeared somber in the late afternoon as snow clouds loomed low through the small six-paned window. The scent of her room reminded me of the mercurochrome and iodine Mom would blot on my scrapes. Mom kissed her Mother's forehead and pulled me close. I touched Mémère's heavily veined and wrinkled hand and said, "Mois lem tui, tui lem mois" and she smiled. I don't remember leaving the room. I do remember the ride home. I felt a heartache that I had never known. That was the last time I saw my beloved Mémère. She passed that evening.

After Mémère was laid to rest, my huge family gathered at our home. Funerals, weddings, births, holidays, graduations, hunting trips, anniversaries or even a new washing machine would give license to gather, feast, and of course, drink. This sad occasion was one I remembered all too well.

Our little house bulged with people. There were tears, laughter and many stories told in a tangled mesh of French and English. From the braided rug to the yellow tinged plaster ceiling, voices swirled in the blue and gray haze of cigarette and pipe smoke. Aunts, uncles, cousins and friends filled the molecules of the house. Food covered every surface of the kitchen and aromas of roasted turkeys and tourtière pies traveled over the smoky waves. I saw sadness in the eyes of the people I loved. I wanted them to not hurt. Having done nothing like this ever before, I donned my Dad's Sunday go-to-Mass fedora, inched my way to the middle of the living room rug and began to do an impersonation of Red Skelton. The gigs of "Gertrude and Heathcliff" and the mimicking of an intoxicated hobo saying "Hey Mr. Dunaheeeee" brought the room to resounding laughter. Everyone tried to squeeze into the space of that blue hazed living room to see what was so comical. I was pumped and the crowd was, too. My facial expressions, body movements and one liners continued; as practiced as pitching fastballs, they just kept coming. The cloud of sadness had been lifted, at least for a while. I had found that I could make sadness go away from other people with comedy.

After Mémère passed Aunt Ida moved into an apartment in Waterville. I would go stay with her sometimes when she was on vacation from work, usually in the summer. She worked at the Hathaway shirt factory stitching mens collars on shirts. She did this work over thirty years. This is when I got to know her friend Arnold. He was a supervisor at that shirt factory and that is how they met. They would take me to watch baseball games in town on summer nights and we would picnic at the goldfish pond on the campus of Colby College. Arnold and a buddy had a camp on Sibley Pond just north of Fairfield, up route 201. I would spend hours in the water or near the water. He is the one who taught me how to water ski. We would go for rides in the boat, go fishing for some dinner and finish the days sitting by a campfire. I really enjoyed those times at camp. I remember cousine Doreen being there a few times as well but not always.

I have good memories of growing up with my siblings. Dan was six years older than I; a quiet boy who needed to have things in order. He had his own bedroom and would play with his fire truck and train set or work on his stamp collection. He would absolutely know if I had touched them or even entered his space. Everything was in its place and I would have been the only one to move them. He didn't shout, yell, or push; he would just say "Don't touch my things unless you ask." He never gave Mom and Dad a problem. I never ever once even heard them scold him. He had his usual boy chores; take out the trash, help shovel snow or mow the lawn but the one I remember him doing the most was his Saturday ritual of going downstairs in the basement where

Dad had a workshop. Dan would collect the family's church shoes, take them downstairs and proceed to polish every shoe until they looked brand new. The swirls of black, brown and sometimes white polish would fill in the cracks of the well worn leather. Dan whisked the soft cloth rhythmically across each stitched layer until the snap of the cloth signaled they were ready for Sunday mass. He walked Lucy and me to school everyday. I am not sure if Mom and Dad told him to take care of us, but I always felt that he was doing just that. He was my big brother and I was happy he was. We attended St. Mary's Parochial Elementary School that was housed in an old three-story wooden building. Our teachers were nuns belonging to the order of the Sisters of Mercy. That old school was not far from the brown and yellow two story apartment house on the south side of the city, but it was a few more miles away from our new home on the east side. When I was entering sixth grade, that school was moved to a newly built brick building directly behind our family parish, on the west side of the city. We were now required to wear a school uniform which was navy blue jumper over a white blouse with a navy blue ribbon tie. I didn't mind it so much because now we all looked the same.

I have fond memories of time with Dan sitting at our local airport on the weekend watching planes take off and land. He always loved planes and dreamed of being a pilot. On some Saturday mornings or late weekday afternoons we would watch cartoons, even catch a run of the Three Stooges. Once in a while I was allowed to stay up and watch the Twilight Zone with him on Saturday night. In later years, the two of us would do car trips to Sugarloaf or some other ski area. I would do imitations of Huckleberry Hound, Boo Boo, Yogi, Moe, Curly and Larry; it kept us in stitches. Dan was not athletic by my standards but he worked hard at learning how to downhill ski. He always tried hard at everything he did.

One Christmas Santa brought Dan a camera. He took to that like I took to playing baseball. He was a natural and began looking at life through a lens. He would take pictures at family holiday gatherings, life events and the natural world. As he got older, with better camera equipment and photography skills, his works of art capturing sunrises over Acadia National Parks rocky coasts were exceptional. Dan was tall, lean-framed with thin fine hands and feet, much like Mom's.

Lucy was my elder by three years. We shared a bedroom, a closet and had the usual squabbling about whose space belonged to whom or whose turn it was to do whatever. A time or two it got physical. I would punch and she would dig with her well- groomed fingernails. It never lasted long. Mom or Dad would intervene and I was the one who ended up on my knees in the corner of the living room, my face to the wall for what seemed like eternity. This was their version of "time out." I never once saw Dan or Lucy there. Boredom would quickly drive my eye to the seam in the wallpaper. Prying tiny rips in that seam would combat my boredom. It went unnoticed for a short while. Let me just say this, it was not a smart thing to do when your Dad's business was wallpapering and painting! From then on, a pair of rosary beads would be handed to me as I occupied that corner. Lucy was an avid fan of the show American Bandstand that was on TV. I recall being asked or pulled into being her dance partner on more than a few occasions. She would announce that I would be the boy. It became fun and we both mastered jitterbugging pretty well.

My sister, like Mom and Dad, had a beautiful voice. It must have been in the genes. She would sing as she did her chores and my memory of her singing me to sleep is one I treasure. We both became members of the children's church choir. She was a soprano and I was more alto. She stayed with it; I dropped out. Lucy was a good girl and was very helpful to Mom cleaning and picking up things. Her Saturday chore was housecleaning and Mom was a good teacher. Both she and Dan were getting small allowances for their chores and they did them faithfully. I, on the other hand, worked at ways to get out of doing any chores in the house. I did them, but not necessarily well enough for Mom or Lucy's trained eye. Washing and drying dishes after supper was the task that Lucy and I had engraved with our names. She would wash, I would dry, not without some words between us. Dad would be sitting in his living room chair watching the nightly news with Chet Huntley and David Brinkley and tell us to "quiet down." We would immediately be silent but our body language and facial movements back and forth kept it all going. Sometimes what started as a quarrel ended up with us in loud fits of laughter. We would hear the familiar "quiet down" but that would only cause us to laugh more, kind of like when you start laughing in church. The harder we tried to stop, the more we laughed until one of us would have to run to another room.

We waited to be excused from the supper table. I remember being excused and running for my ball and glove; straight out the door I would go to the neighborhood empty lot hoping to get a game going. "Jackie get back here," would be the call from my sister, to no avail. "Jackie get back here now," was the bellow from my Dad that had great success. The supper dishes would be waiting for me.

Lucy was not athletic. Her eye/hand coordination needed a little work. Trying to hit or catch a ball was not her thing but she could ice skate well. She made smooth circles and backwards skating look easy. Time spent with her at the public rink on cold winter Saturdays is a good memory.

She always wanted to learn to play the piano but never had the opportunity. Lucy had slender shoulders, a small waist with broad hips and thick legs and feet, much like Dad and his sisters.

The three of us were average students and school work every afternoon and evening during the week was a regular routine. Each one of us wrestled with some subject but we persevered. Both Mom and Dad knew the importance of education and would give us pointers when they could. Mom had to stay home and help raise her younger siblings so she never got to finish grade school and Dad did have the opportunity to attend a college for a few years.

We kids began looking for ways to earn money as soon as we could. We could see that working for the things you may need or want was how life went. I was always thankful for the solid work ethic Mom and Dad taught us. Dan had an early morning newspaper route. He would sling a large canvas bag stuffed with newspapers across his body, jump on his red bike and be gone. Winter was a slow slog by foot over ice or snow-covered roads. On Friday afternoons he would have to make his way around his route to collect payment for his deliveries, always hoping for a good tip for his work. He spent a little time as a bellboy at Mom's hotel running people up and down an old Otis elevator with a hand-held lever to start or stop the cage at floor level. It took practice to land that moving elevator right at the perfect spot so no one had to step up or down. There were no push buttons to do that job back then. Lucy would babysit and she loved it. She was in demand. I, on the other hand, was offered by Mom to babysit a few times. I would resist, plead, but it made no difference. I did not want to take care of little kids. Finally, after a few times of having to call Mom for backup assistance, she stopped offering me up.

Fall and Spring cleaning of our home were rituals that Dan managed to never be part of and I figured out it was because he was a boy. Deep cleaning was "women's work." I didn't think it was fair then and deeply believe it is not fair now. My sister and I would have the chore of doing not only our home but for a number of years we would be driven over to my Dad's elderly Aunt Emily and Uncle Len's on the west side of the city on a Saturday to do their twice yearly deep cleaning of their old home. I looked forward to my Saturdays with great anticipation and giving them up to clean dark brown baseboards, crown molding and everything in between was not what I wanted to spend my time doing. There was no fun in it and it was as boring to me as watching paint dry. Aunt Emily was a stern old lady. They had never had children; there was no soft and fuzzy anything radiating from her. Facial crevasses so deeply-carved into her face shielded any chance of an escaping smile. Uncle Len smiled through his soft gleaming eyes and was quick to hug. We were paid well for our efforts but I still wanted my Saturday back.

Lucy started working for Mom waitressing when she was sixteen. I was to be the "Relish Girl" on holidays until I was old enough to work. Mom always told us that "If you learn to wait tables well and correctly you will never have to worry about starving." I started collecting returnable bottles and cans from neighbors and would cart them to the mom-and-pop store a few blocks away. Shoveling a few walks and clearing some driveway entrances of plowed snow banks would earn me a little more cash. This stash was the downpayment for a bike. Dan had his bike. I don't remember Lucy having one, but I sure wanted one and I wanted it to look just like my brother's red one.

One Spring Saturday Dad took me to the second-hand shop on Bangor Street where he had picked one out for me. I carried my coins and cash in a small brown paper bag into the store. I was getting a bike and could barely wait to get shopping when my eye caught the one I wanted standing just inside the door. Dad walked over to the one he had picked out. I did not know that he had already negotiated with the owner. Dad's choice was a white and orange bike with no crossbar in the middle; a girl's bike. I never showed my disappointment. I handed the money bag over to the man.

That was my first purchase of anything that I had worked for. That bike took me on miles and miles of adventurous trips all over the city of Augusta, but I always longed for that red boy's bike.

When I was sixteen I began working for Mom and learning how to wait tables properly. When we were not actually waiting on tables we would be filling salt and pepper shakers, folding linen napkins, tablecloths and polishing silverware that seemed to never end. This was one of many jobs I would gain experience from. Lucy was an excellent waitress and made good tips. I did okay, but the lesson it really taught me was that I did not want to do that kind of work for a living. I much preferred showing a friend how to stand at home plate than placing and removing a plate in front of someone from the right or the left. Being outdoors doing anything was far and away a better fit for me.

Dan graduated from high school and went to college in Nova Scotia for a year. He struggled in the engineering program and did not return. The draft was going to claim him. The Vietnam war was on and he wanted to be a pilot. He enlisted in the Air Force, found out he was color blind and his dream of being a pilot ended. While in the military he worked on the flight deck under the belly of aircrafts checking for electrical issues. When he was sent to Thailand we all breathed a sigh of relief that he was not any closer to the actual war. Years later he would complete undergraduate and graduate work and have a career in the recruitment of engineers. Dan married his wife Jane, an ex-nun, and soon left Maine to begin their new lives and raise their daughter. Lucy finished high school and went on to get a licensed practical nursing certificate. She worked a few years in local hospitals until she married Will and they started a family. Years later when their children were in school Lucy went back to using her nursing skills in a seniors facility. When she and Will became empty nesters she started a new career as manager in a dental office. Lucy was made to be a mom. I remember her as a teenager talking about wanting a dozen kids. All her babysitting experiences had prepared her well. She was a good mother and juggled family life with three young ones well. Both she and Will had discovered the reality of having and raising kids; they stopped having children after three. Those three kids would be the children I would never have. I loved them as a mother loves a child. Being allowed to help raise them was one of the greatest gifts in my life. Frequent trips to their home in New Hampshire were common. Through the years they would spend a week or just weekends with me during the summer and school vacations. Staying with Aunt Jackie was something they looked forward to. I of course would spoil them anyway that I could. Late bedtimes were the rule. Huge piles of pillows mounded on the livingroom floor was the perfect place to launch themselves into; their giggles and laughter covered the walls of my home like a meadow of wildflowers poured into a vase. Shopping trips with bags of new outfits, sneakers and a toy or two would be laid out and packed up for their return home. The adventures of helping them learn to throw a ball, swim, ski, ice fish, and ride a bike are memories that will always make me smile. I tried to stay in their lives as they grew and by the time they were teenagers it became more difficult. It was no longer cool to come spend time with AJ; they had new roads to discover. I missed them then and I miss them now. They are all adults who have raised children of their own. My time with their children has been very limited. Living in different States kept us apart but I always made steady attempts to stay connected to all of them. My life would not have been nearly so enriched had I not thought of them as my kids.

DIFFERENT

By the time I was seven or eight years old I knew I was different from other little girls. I certainly fit the definition of a TomBoy. Running, leaping, throwing, catching and hitting a ball was as natural to me as a sleeping dog stretching back into a tucked curl. I excelled at playing many sports; basketball, baseball, football, volleyball, tennis, golf, and downhill skiing. I was proficient in motor skills and because I was, I loved using them. I was agile and quick for my size. By the time I was in double digits I wanted to be a professional baseball player. I dreamed it; slept with my glove and knew the well-worn leather would only make more great plays during the next game. Most of the time I was the only girl on the neighborhood teams. I was usually the first one picked but I could see what a kid felt like when they were the last one chosen for a team. Home runs were frequent; so were broken windows in Mr. Gage's garage. This was the era before well- intentioned adults took over the joys of children's play. We had no parent umpires or referees and no parent spectators. We set our own rules, adapted our games and learned to work out the squabbles that came from a bad call. The confidence and skills I learned playing these games laid a solid foundation that I relied on my entire life. I knew the value of what sport was intended to teach. I liked playing by the rules in sports and I played by them. I later met the rules of the "good old boys club" and refused to play by their rules.

I had girl friends and boy friends and much preferred spending time with the guys. A sharp shooter hanging off my hip and cowboy boots on my feet belonged. Chiffon dresses with petticoats, dressing and undressing dolls did not. I never experienced happiness playing with a doll but would pretend to. I tried to fit in to whatever position I found myself placed in. Getting all dressed up to attend a little girlfriend's birthday party was a chore but Mom made sure I did it. I wanted to go be with friends but I didn't want to wear a frilly dress. I was out of place, like a minnow seizing to catch a breath on a rocky shore. I began to think I should have been born a boy, but of course never ever spoke that thought to anyone. It was my secret and I knew how to keep a secret.

After multiple pleadings with Mom I got a pair of stiff dungarees. From the first time I zipped them up from the front instead of zipping up slacks from the side I knew I belonged in them. I couldn't wait to get home from school and slide into those dungarees with rolled-up cuffs and grass-stained knees. I would have lived in those pants but I knew that couldn't happen; I had to keep working so I would fit in.

My baby fat was replaced with plain chubbiness. Dan would call me Baby Huey now and again. I knew it was in fun but it still pinched. The first time I heard an uncle call me "a little fatty" the pinch was replaced with a sting. That uncle was a horrible tease and would tease his nieces and his own daughters until they would cry. I never cried in front of him, but my heart hurt for my teased cousin's obvious pain. He stopped teasing me and I believe to this day it was because I would ignore him. He remained an unmerciful tease until there were no more little girls. This was the beginning of my learning how to react to taunting, bullying and name-calling. I would put any hurt feelings inside of me where they would stay frozen, like ice cubes. They wouldn't touch me. I was chubby, tall, sported short hair and was known as a TomBoy. I saw myself as the black sheep of our family and my self image was that of a potato with toothpicks sticking out. My broad shoulders, long thin arms and legs did not seem to fit the rest of me. I wore dungarees and wanted to wear a baseball cap more than any girl should, but I didn't dare. I was sometimes mistaken for a boy as it was, and, had I given in, it would have only made my life more difficult. I began looking into the mirror that hung on the wall over the dresser that Lucy and I shared in our bedroom and would say to myself "You're a good person, just different; you're okay." That became my mantra until my early forties. This was a routine I would repeat hundreds and hundreds of times in my life as I prepared for school or work. A baseball cap would always occupy a special space on my shelf and by my mid-forties it had been well worn and faded with a ragged visor. I was learning how to be compliant with the outside world but my insides were slowly brewing into a Nor'easter.

Mom buying me my first bra was nowhere near as exciting for me as getting my dungarees. Some facts of life told to me by my older sister took the place of any Mom should have told me. I just don't remember Mom giving me "the talk." The arrival of my period was in no way celebratory and finding out that I would have to deal with it every month for many years just added to my unhappiness. Mom smiled at me and gave me a hug. Dad said "My little girl is a young lady now." I guess I was a young lady but would always see myself as a TomBoy.

One morning I was getting ready to go to school. I slipped my navy blue school jumper over my head and when I pulled it down over my shoulders I was staring into the mirror. Images of my bedroom that were reflected in the mirror looked like they were all moving in slow motion. My bed was gyrating up and down as if on a wave. The rug where my dog slept was rising and falling as the floor did a slow pivot. I began to move about the room quickly, but pulling up my knee socks and putting on my shoes all seemed like I was doing it in slow motion. I kept my head down, talked to myself and just kept moving. I was more than freaked out; I was frightened. I thought I was going crazy. It lasted only a few minutes but in my mind it lasted a long time. I was afraid that it would happen again. It did return a few more times and each time it left me fearful. I never told anyone; I thought they would think I was nuts. My mantra was now recited daily. I believed it would keep the "slows" as I referred to them, away. Later in life I learned these were anxiety attacks.

My best friend Marilyn and her family had moved from the brown and yellow two-story apartment building on the south side of the city to the east side, closer to me. Her cousin Tess, however, would remain living in that building until she left for college. Tess's parents owned it. Mom and Tess's mom, Celia, were friends. From my house to Marilyn's house, by way of walking streets, was a few miles long and down and up some steep hills. There was a large section of privately-owned woods that we soon learned we could cut through. It made the walk much easier and shorter. We used it often and never feared to walk it alone unless it was near dark. Those woods were darker than a pocket after sunset. I was not a fan of the dark, ever. I wasn't one to hide in closets or dark basements playing tag or hide and seek. If I had to, I always made sure I had a flashlight.

Marilyn attended the same Catholic elementary school on the southwest side of the city, St. Marys. We were good friends but very different. She didn't play ball but I do remember bouncing a little pinky ball back and forth with her in the driveway. She had long blond hair, sometimes polished nails and always wore coordinated clothes that were ironed with creases in sleeves and collars. She was intelligent and had perfect Palmer Method penmanship, but then most children who attended school taught by nuns had good penmanship. I learned good study skills from Marilyn and she was helpful, particularly when we got to high school. I was not an abstract thinker. I was a visual tactile learner so I trudged along.

There was another Catholic school, attached to a Catholic church on the northside of the city situated at the top of a hill. St. Augustine overlooked the local woolen mill that sat on the banks of the Kennebec river. That area was referred to as "French town" or "The Hill." Families of Franco-American dissent migrated to that section of the city when they moved south from New Brunswick, the Province of Quebec or northern Maine. Masses were said in the Acadian French dialect. The French-speaking order of nuns were the Sisters of the Presentation, who taught school. Mémère's youngest daughter was a member of that order for a number of years. This is where Tess went to school. "The Hill" was often referred to in an unkind way. The large French families were often discriminated against and looked upon as poor and uneducated. Both Mom and Dad had lived on "The Hill" and I believe they made a willful decision to not raise their family there. I had many aunts, uncles and cousins who called that area home. That is where my Mémère lived until she moved up river in 1955 to Waterville.

SAINT MARY'S SCHOOL

I have mostly good memories of my sixth, seventh and eighth grade years in our new school. Sister Immaculata was short, of Latin American descent, spoke softly but with authority. She was my teacher in sixth grade and moved up to be the seventh grade teacher right along with us. She knew us and we knew her. We never heard her coming. She seemed to glide over the floor, not even her long oversized rosary beads would give her away, unlike so many of the other sisters that swished and clanged as they moved about.

One day she gave us a homework assignment to use the Punnett Square that we had worked with in science class. She wanted us to draw up the square, plug in our parents' eye colors and see the probability of what eye colors their children would have. I was sitting at the kitchen table before supper time working on my homework. Mom was standing at the kitchen sink with a candle, burning some scraggly feathers off a chicken that she was preparing for supper. Both she and Dad had brown eyes. I began to plug in the information. The way I was working the square it showed my sister and brother having dark eyes, which they had, but nowhere on that square could I find a place that showed much of a probability of a blue-eyed child. I had blue eyes. After repeatedly trying to complete the square, in frustration, I said to Mom "I just can't get this to work; I must be doing something wrong. I can't get a blue-eyed square. Did you guys adopt me?" Mom looked into the round mirror over the sink, never turned her face and laughed her little nervous chuckle. "Of course not dear, just ask Sister Immaculata for help." The next day I did just that. With a slight pat on my shoulder Immaculata said "Sometimes these things just don't work out, dear." I was thrilled that my homework was not looked upon as undone or unfinished and never gave it another thought. I would never know if Mom made a call to that nun to explain anything.

Aunt Ida's daughter Doreen was graduating from the private Waterville Catholic high school that she had attended as a day student. My family was invited to go to the ceremony as Aunt Ida and Doreen had been frequent visitors and Doreen and my sister Lucy were good friends. That high school sat next to the boarding school, elementary school and convent that was all housed in the same three and a half story old wooden building that was adjacent to the brick one story high school. The Ursuline Sisters were the order that ran both the boarding school and the high school. We went to the graduation and attended a small family gathering at Ida's apartment. On the ride back home Mom asked me if that might be a place I might like to go to high school as a day student. I was impressed with the place and the ceremony; I gave Mom a definite maybe. I knew going to a private school cost money. I also knew that was something our family did not have. I never wondered why this was being offered to me and not my sister until many years later. In fact, I was asked by cousin Doreen to do some babysitting for her and her husband when I was in my teens. Doreen had told her kids to call me Aunt Jackie. I never gave it a thought.

Our Parish had purchased a nine-passenger station wagon that was used during the week for some parish girls to drive and attend that Waterville Catholic girls' high school twenty-five miles away, as day students. Marilyn told me she was going to be one of the girls. She was a year ahead of me.

As time went on Marilyn told me she liked it. I told Mom that she liked going to school there and that I would like to go. I was excited about being able to still go to high school with my best friend.

FALL 1964

A green wool blazer, emblem stitched on the left pocket, white short sleeved blouse, grey wool skirt with one-inch pleats, grey knee socks and brown and white saddle shoes was the uniform that I would wear every school day of my high school life. Green beret caps were worn for Masses and special occasions along with nylons and black high heels. I felt special in that uniform and was thankful the nylons and heels were not an everyday thing.

Bernice was in her junior year and was the one who would pick us up and drive us to school my freshmen year. There were eight of us in that light blue, push-button Plymouth station wagon. Marilyn, myself, and another girl named Pam would sit in the way back seat that faced backwards. Pam lived on "The Hill" and was Franco-American. French was spoken at home, some English too. She was a good ball player and preferred to play outdoors, like me. She wore her uniform skirt low on her hips and always had a shirt tail untucked until of course, Mother Agustus would catch a glimpse and Pam would quietly be instructed to "tuck it in please." The three of us became solid friends. I finally met a girl who liked to do the things that I liked to do.

I was enrolled in college-bound course work but struggled with Math. I always had. From the time fractions entered my life in elementary school Math would be my nemesis. The summer going into my junior year Mother Agustus sent my parents a letter to say that because of my math grades they would be changing me from college-bound courses to commercial courses. I protested. I told her and my parents I wanted to go to college and would work harder or get help. Agustus told me, in her low, slow voice, "You are not smart enough to go to college." It didn't matter what I said and with no intervention from my parents I was put into commercial courses. Typing, shorthand, bookkeeping and filing is how I spent my last two years. I was miserable and had absolutely no desire to sit at a desk and be some guy's secretary. I was more determined than ever to go to college.

By the time school began in September of my junior year my Dad's Uncle Len had come to live with us. Aunt Emily had recently died and he could no longer manage living on his own in their large house. Their home and belongings were sold. That year I was the one designated to be the driver of that light blue nine passenger push-button Plymouth station wagon. On a dark and rainy October afternoon we were headed for home and had just left the school parking lot. Everyone was getting settled in when the station wagon rounded a curve onto a leaf-soaked bridge. The station wagon hydroplaned and we were hit from both sides; one car coming towards us and one behind us. We were all in school uniforms; there was no doubt where we had just come from. I stepped out of the car into the rain and checked to see if anyone was hurt. I saw a few bumps and bruises, a couple small cuts but no one seemed to be in pain; all just pretty shaken up. In a matter of minutes a couple of our school nuns were on the scene and two of the girls were transported to the hospital to be checked. We were taken back to the high school where parents were called. Two of the girls' mothers showed up to take the rest of us back home. Within a week plans had been made to drive some of the girls to school and some went from being day students to boarding school students. Marilyn and Pam would continue to be day students; it was their senior year. I became a boarder and life as I had known it changed overnight.

I knew some of the boarding school girls from classes but had not hung out with them. There was a clear social division between the day students and the boarding students. I seldom got to see Marilyn and Pam anymore, except during school and summer vacations. I later learned from Mom the reason I was able to become a boarding student was because of Uncle Len's generosity by giving Mom and Dad money. Aunt Ida lived in the same town and volunteered to do my laundry so that my folks would not have to pay that extra fee. She would drop my laundry off in the silver metal laundry boxes we all had and at times would ask to see me briefly or invite me to come over for her cacciatore.

I made friends easily but was thrown into a Catholic life of daily Masses, weekly confessions and dining room meals in silence until a nun would pronounce a blessing; we would dutifully respond and then we could speak softly at our table. We had to sit and wait for all to finish before we could be excused. I had good table manners; Mom and Dad made sure of that. I sat up straight, had no elbows on the table and never rested my arms anywhere but on my lap. I held my eating utensils correctly and placed them on the plate as I was taught.

The three and a half story boarding school was very old. Wooden floors creaked, railings were loose, plaster walls had cracks, enameled sinks had rusted drip marks and bathtubs wore permanent rings. Small single light bulb fixtures attached to beadboard ceilings made for a dark physical space.

I think there were about thirty of us as I recall. Most were in dorms with five to eight beds. There were a couple of semi-private rooms and a few private rooms. The boarding school occupied the second floor, the elementary school was on the first floor and the refectory, kitchen, study hall and chapel were in what, to me, looked like a renovated basement. We had four individual bathtubs each placed in small private closets on our main floor and four individual wooden shower stalls up on the third floor that we shared with the nuns. Our bathing time was between seven o'clock and nine o'clock only. We had to sign up for either a shower or a tub at a designated time and we were given fifteen minutes to do whatever needed to be done. Lights were to be turned out by ten o'clock. Many of us would continue studying under our blankets using flashlights. Some of the girls wanted to switch a shower for a tub once in a while; it wasn't a problem, but that fifteen minutes was always too short.

My senior year I was elected president of the boarding school; I never ran for it. I would listen to the concerns of the girls, asked for more frequent tv nights, less turnips to eat and more outdoor time. Our Mother mistress would listen and sometimes make an adjustment. Outwardly it appeared that I was adjusting well. I even chose to stay at the boarding school on weekends. No one knew that I chose to stay because it kept me from seeing my Dad drunk. Inside I felt lost and lonely, as lost as the time I got turned around in the woods when I was hunting with my Dad. I got out of those woods because I trusted my compass. I had no compass to which to refer. I felt fear and I was not able to understand or identify why. Studying became difficult, completing school work became difficult and I had to resolve that my dungarees, baseballs and gloves were things of the past.

One Saturday afternoon I took a razor blade, walked into the bathroom, stood over a sink and proceeded to put a ten-inch cut into the top of my right arm. Rich red blood dripped into the old white chipped sink. A girl came in, saw the blood and went running to find our boarding school mistress, Mother Mary Ellen. I remember the sound of her rustling habit and the pounding of my heart in my ears when I heard her exclaim "What happened?" I proceeded to contrive some story about a razor blade being stuck in the seam of an old mattress that I was turning over. I was taken to a doctor, staples were put in my arm and I returned to the boarding school. I know Mom was called but I have no idea what was said and Mom never said anything to me about the incident. What I do know for sure was that the following weekend Mom came to the boarding school and both she and Mother Mary Ellen met in Mother Mary Ellen's small bedroom that was in the middle of one of the long dark hallways.

A week later Mother Mary Ellen called me into her small room and asked me quietly how I was. Was there anything I wanted to talk about? I just shrugged my shoulders and said "No, not now." It was the first time anyone had ever asked me those questions. I had no idea how to answer. I was not able to say how I felt because I did not let myself feel. This was the beginning of a long and trusted friendship that I had with this nun. She became my confidant and I would be forever grateful for her support and care. She believed in me and told me so. In that senior year I had one more cutting incident. Years later I learned through counseling and therapy why those cuttings occurred. For me, it had nothing to do with wanting attention as so many people believed. It was a way to release the glacier of frozen feelings and guilt that had been built inside of me.

I was not accepted into college upon graduating from high school due to my lack of college prep course work. I needed to be able to demonstrate that I could do the work. So, in the Fall, I enrolled in a local community college and took courses that I needed so that I could apply to a four-year degree program. I was working full time in the meat room of a grocery store and soon went from wrapping meat and fish to cutting meat and fish. I acquired lifelong skills as a card-carrying member of the Amalgamated Meat Cutters Union. Wednesdays were fish days and boxes of iced fish needed to be cut, filleted and packaged. I would work until mid afternoon and drive straight to my college class. No one sat next to me; there was no amount of body spray that would kill the fishy smell. Thankfully, I was able to laugh about it and so did my classmates; I was grateful. That was but one of many blue collar jobs I would tackle. In late winter I began to apply to a couple of colleges. I wanted to major in physical educa-tion; I wanted to teach and coach. By mid-summer I still had not been accepted anywhere. I had known that Mom and Dad could not afford to pay for me to go to school. I knew I would have to work but even that wouldn't be enough. My brother Dan had gone through the process of obtaining a college loan and thanks to his guidance and effort I was able to secure one. In mid-August I got a letter from Aroostcock State Teachers College in Northern Maine. They would accept me into the Fall semester in their HPER (Health, Physical Education and Recreation) program on a trial basis. I would be placed on probation and if I was successful in doing that semester's work requirements I could remain in school. I was going to college.

1969

College is where I learned it was not only okay to question but expected for you to question. I heard young men and young women speaking more than just French and English. I saw people of different color and varied dress. Most of all, I saw young women doing the things I liked and doing them very well. They were athletic, strong and determined. Some had been tagged as lesbians just because of those qualities, some had not. I worked hard to be one who had not.

I was now able to choose to not attend Sunday Mass, or not eat meat on Fridays. I had spent my short life being told that I would carry sins (mortal sins would send me to hell) if I did the things that they told me were bad and had been ingrained in me from the time I made my first communion. I will never forget being eleven years old, playing at a friend's house on a Friday and being invited for supper. They were having grilled chicken; the smell to me was intoxicating. I remember calling home and asking if I could stay for supper. When Dad asked what they were having I told him they were having fish sticks. I knew that lie and the guilt of eating meat would put me in hell for sure but I did it anyway. I carried extra guilt all week until I could clear the sin on Saturday when we went to confession. Guilt and the weight it carried was learned early on. It would be a difficult weight to ever lose.

I dated two young men while I was in college. Applying myself to my studies, being an interscholastic athlete and working off campus left me little time for social activity. There were the Saturday night dates to the local bar and dance club, usually with my roommate and her date. Those evenings would end with some making out. I never let anything ever go much past second base. My body had been awakened to adult urges back in eighth grade. A friend's high school age brother and I had done the kissy face, body-exploring thing. The panting, hot breath and squirming, to me, was more like an octopus groping for a tasty morsel that was clinging to a barnacled quahog.

We would hear rumors about roommates in the dorm or women on our teams being lesbians. We heard the same rumors about guys in their dorms but mostly about guys in the actors studio, never about guys on any teams. I did not like to hear the word lesbian, gay was softer to my ears, or so it seemed. I was in college the first time when I was directly asked if I was gay. My denial was swift and deep. I did not see myself as a gay person. I didn't look at women's bodies in a sexual way; in fact, I liked looking at men's toned muscular bodies more. I had made emotional attachments with a few girlfriends through the years. I never thought of having any sexual experience with them.

The man I had been dating for about a year was employed at a local wood furniture factory. I liked him very much. He smelled of wood chips, had calloused hands and bulging forearms. Over time, he told me he loved me. I did not return the sentiment. I knew I loved my family, loved my dog, loved my stuffed animals. I could not say I knew romantic love. I wasn't seeing twinkling stars and had not experienced any heart fluttering when I thought of him. I wasn't able to acknowledge or identify feelings; they had been frozen within, out of my reach or touch. It would be decades later before any internal warmth would begin the slow melt of those stacking ice cubes.

In the days ahead I thought about Marc, what he said. I looked at things with him as a practical matter; we had fun. I had no thoughts of marriage. If we got married I saw myself staying in northern Maine and having kids while he worked. That would be my life. I had worked hard and wanted to have a career in teaching and coaching. Having children then was not my priority. I just didn't see it working out, for either of us. Just before Thanksgiving of my final semester, we were in his car and I told him we needed to talk. He said he had some things he wanted to say and to ask me. I did not give him the chance.

I put my hand up and said I think it best that we not see each other anymore. I told him we had fun times and enjoyed each other's company but that I wanted my career and did not know where that would take me. He was sad. I got out of the car and never saw him again.

I had made the Dean's List my last two years of college. Aroostook State College had become part of the University of Maine and I was pleased to be part of that University. Upon my graduation in December I sent an announcement of the ceremony to Mother Agustus who had told me I was not smart enough to go to college. The note simply read "And you said it couldn't be done."

JANUARY 1973

I was ready and eager to start my teaching career. I knew getting a teaching job in January might prove to be difficult. I was fortunate and received three offers to teach and coach at Maine Public High Schools. I made my decision based on who I would be working with. I knew my male counterpart was a well- respected, longtime physical educator and coach who could teach me years worth of practical experiences in a short time. The integration of co-ed physical education had not happened yet at that school.

I was told by the superintendent during my interview that the program had little structure. Girls were not required to wear gym shorts or tee shirts and they didn't have to participate if they didn't want to. The administration was looking for a solid physical education curriculum to be implemented. I knew I would have my work cut out for me. My thoughts were I would stay at this school for five or six years, get some experience and move on.

Within the first two weeks my first real challenge arrived. One afternoon, right after dismissal, a few junior and senior girls came into the locker room. I was putting things up on a bulletin board outside of my office. They circled me and began to say that they were going to continue to do whatever they wanted and that "no queer" was going to change the way things had been done. They never touched me; I never touched them. I told them they needed to leave and when they didn't move I made my way out of the locker room's back door. Visibly shaken, I arrived in the Principal's office and told him what had just happened. I further said to him "I don't want you to do anything, not now. I will handle this and if I need your support I will let you know; I just wanted you to be aware."

The following day a large note on the locker room bulletin board said "Don't change up, just have a seat on the benches." So began what for years would be referred to as "Ms. P.'s locker room chats." I explained to each class that day that I knew changes would not be easy at first and that I would listen to their concerns. I would move slowly, but, the expectations were going to require them to move, practice and learn new motor skills and that meant they would have to change into shorts and t-shirts; no more wearing street clothes for gym class. By the time that school year ended things had smoothed out. I always told students that it was cool to be a good student, to work hard and to look ahead. Their high school life would be over soon. I would encourage them to get more education after high school and to dream about what and where they might see their lives going.

One junior boy I remember well would try to get out of gym class so that he could stay in the shop and work on a car. I told him that I could see he really loved doing that kind of work and asked him what he wanted to do after high school. He told me he wanted to be a mechanic. I told him to think about not only being a mechanic but asked him to think about having and running his own business. He would have to be willing to go on to a voc tech school to learn all he could about doing just that. I will never forget the look in his eyes when he began to think that he could possibly do just that. A dozen years later I got a note from him. He was a mechanic and had just started his own shop with another guy. It made my heart smile. Girls would look at me in panic to tell me they thought they were pregnant; some were. I would encourage them to tell their parent or parents as soon as possible and that I would help them do that if they needed support. Other girls would hug me in relief because they started their periods. I had many conversations with boys and girls over the years about not ruining their young lives for five minutes of sexual pleasure. I was a student advocate and they knew it.

In those days every student in the high school had P.E. class every day. Gym classes were very large, a downside for teaching. I got to know every kid in that school, an upside for me. I was able to relate to the emotional turmoil of my students. I would encourage, listen and remind them that there was a big world outside of their small town; that the factories and the mill probably would not always be there for them to rely on. They would hear me say over and over that education would give them choices and choices were empowering and if they wanted it badly enough they could achieve it but it would take work.

From the very beginning of my work in that school I saw the inequity of girls sports compared with the boys. The discrimination between the male and female programs was glaring. We would get little gym time for practices and if we got any it would be after the guys practiced, often late in the evening. We had less than adequate equipment, four basketballs to their 12 and one set of well-worn uniforms while the boys teams had home and away outfits. The male coaches' salaries were at least three and sometimes four times more than the female coaches. It was not right and it was not fair. After a couple years presenting case after case of these discrepancies to my athletic director and the high school's administration, it made no difference. It was falling on deaf ears. I knew I had entered the "Good old boys" world but refused to play by their rules. Title IX was adopted by Congress in June 1972 as part of the Education Amendments of 1972 and stated " no person in the United States shall, on the basis of sex, be excluded from participation in, be denied the benefits of, or be subjected to discrimination under any education program or activity receiving Federal financial assistance." I called the Maine Human Rights Commission and filed an affirmative action discrimination suit against my teachers' association and my school district for ratifying a contract that was so blatantly discriminatory to girls and women. I tried to get another female coach working at my school to do this with me but she would not. She was fearful of losing her job. An investigator was sent to the school to do interviews. It did not take long for the results to be in. The investigator met with the principal and superintendent. The next day I was called to meet with the superintendent. He knew that the school department would not win this lawsuit; he also knew that I had the right to request back pay for the previous two years. He asked "What is it you want?" I told him that from this day forward, all girls programs would be treated equally with their male counterparts; the same equipment and uniform budgets, rotating practice times etc. and that anyone who would coach a girls team, be they male or female, would have the same salary as the men coaching the same sport. No back pay was requested. He shook his head and said "You got it." We shook hands. The suit never went further. I had found my voice. To this day, I still correspond with that ninety-year old superintendent and his wife. I had the pleasure of teaching their children when they were in high school and upon his retirement they returned to their lovely island home in Penobscot Bay where I visited with them and was treated to a tour of the island and some of the best lobster rolls I had ever eaten. I stay in contact with their family and hope that one day we will meet again.

1975

That summer was spent playing softball on a city team in Augusta. There were two games a week and many weekends were spent playing in tournaments around the state. I looked forward to every game. I made some new friends that summer and spent as much time as possible with my nieces and nephew. I would sleep on their couch and be awakened by three little people in pjs tickling my face, laying across my body and snuggling under my arm. Those kids filled my heart. Teaching them to play ball, sleep in a tent and eat ice cream for supper was glorious.

Once in a while I would stay at Mom and Dad's. My teaching friend, Peter, had helped me find a used trailer that I now called home. It was a few miles from my school and about thirty miles from Augusta. When it was time for me to go back to school one friend in particular would drive from the city to my place to visit or stay for supper once or twice a week. We became close friends. She knew I was looking for a roommate to share expenses. Living paycheck to paycheck on a teacher's salary was a way of life. By November she had moved in and had found a job in the local shoe factory.

Dad passed the following June. He had three serious heart attacks since the early sixties with so much muscle damage that repairs of any kind were not an option. I remember seeing him in an oxygen tent back when I was twelve and thought he was going to die, just like my Mémère did. By 1970 he had quit smoking his pipe which had replaced cigarettes after his first attack and had stopped drinking because of health issues. He was the kind, soft Dad that I liked to be around, now even on weekends. I told him so. I told him I was proud of him; that he was a totally different person when he was not drinking. He looked at me and said "Is that so?" We hugged. A good memory for me. Dad retired in May of that year. Mom found him sitting in his lawn chair in the yard one afternoon when she had finished her lunch shift. Mom told me years later that she had been told by his doctor that he would never survive another heart attack and that he knew he did not have much time. After Dad's passing I started going to church again, not sure why, but it felt familiar.

To this day I can't say if it was the grief I was dealing with, the loneliness or the hurt, but a week after Dad's funeral I had my first sexual encounter and yes, it was with my roommate friend. I looked at her and said "What are we doing?" "We can never do that again." So began a duplicitous life that continued over twenty years. Within the confines of our home we lived as a couple but I was emotionally crumbling trying to live two lives. I still did not consider myself gay, not a lesbian. Denial could be a powerful tool to help defray someone's reality. The guilt I carried was devastating to me. We would attend Mass together, be seen in public together but I was always looking over my shoulder. It was not an easy or comfortable existence. I didn't know, accept or love myself so how could I know what I needed or wanted in a relationship? I did not know.

One Thursday afternoon I was approached by a colleague of mine asking if I would consider running for a seat on the parish council. I said I would think about it. Much to my surprise on that next Sunday visit to Mass, there were parish council ballots in every pew and my name was on them. I was elected. The following week I was asked to be a lecturer at Mass. I was comfortable with public speaking, so I agreed. This continued for a number of years. One snowy Sunday morning I was scheduled to lecture at the eight o'clock Mass. No altar boys showed up so I went about getting what I needed out of the sacristy to light the candles on the altar and get the offerings ready. Father began saying Mass, there were a small number of folks in the pews and no one came forth to assist him. I naturally stepped forward to carry the wine and the water to him, handed him a towel when he washed his fingers, rang the bell when the eucharist was blessed and placed the gold disk under the chins of those receiving communion. Mass ended, I went into the sacristy to get what I needed to put the candles out and Father said to me " Do not ever do that again; there is no place for women at the altar." I looked at him and said "Excuse me Father?" He just walked away shaking his head. I was angry, hurt and insulted beyond description. I anguished at being treated like that. I never returned to Mass or to lecture or to any more parish council meetings. When Mom would come visit me I would drop her off at church for Mass but would not go in. She could not understand why I would no longer go to church, she just did not get it, in fact said to me "Why are you doing this to me?" I told her it was not about her. I told her what had happened. Things between me and my God were okay, I knew about forgiveness and my God knew and loved me. I did not need some priest to tell me what I would or would not be allowed to do in practicing my faith. All the falsehoods of the past, the archaic thinking of the men who made up the rules and my knowing that it was the women who did most of the work just was not okay. So began my epic swim toward recovery from Catholic guilt.

One day I was out jogging when a car drove by and someone threw a bottle at me followed by a yell of "you better run faggot." I knew how much sticks and stones could break your bones; I also knew names did harm you. I jogged for weight control and stress relief. I wasn't fast but I enjoyed the workouts. Trips out my front door, down roads and streets would at times be scarred by shouts of "faggot", " queer", "lesbo" coming from a passing car. I would tell myself "You're okay" over and over and continue running.

In those days that blue collar mill town on the banks of the Androscoggin river proved to be pretty typical. It was Italian, French, almost totally vanilla, and very hard-working; a tight community of locals, but not so welcoming to "outsiders" or folks different from themselves. Diversity in that town would be an ongoing slow shift. It would begin to become enlightened but at a snail's pace.

BURNED OUT

At the conclusion of a school year in the 80's I was experiencing what I called teacher burnout. I loved working with kids but teaching motor skills over and over and over became stagnant. I had discovered many new ways to teach the same skills but there were limits. Teaching the mechanics of throwing, catching, hitting, kicking, jumping, running became redundant. I was good at adapting games and movements to acquire mastery of the same skills but I needed to do something totally different for work for a while. I decided to get a part time job doing some kind of manual labor that summer. I was experienced in short stints of manual labor; in a woolen mill, a chicken processing plant, digging sandworms at low tide, waiting tables, short order cook, slinging pizza and beers, and cutting and wrapping meat. As the summer break began I had the opportunity to work a couple days a week delivering ice. By hand, two of us would move hundreds of pounds of ice from a large holding freezer into a smaller delivery truck freezer, stop at convenience stores, fill their freezers, gas stations, fill their freezers etc, until our truck was empty. We would then drive back to the original large holding freezer and begin to once again load our delivery truck. We then continued on our route, unloading it all once again. My hands and body stacked and unstacked hundreds and hundreds of pounds of ice a day. I was in the best shape of my life. By the time school started I was very happy and excited to be teaching motor skills once again. Getting reacquainted with manual labor was just the ticket I needed. Burn out was gone.

I put all my energy and focus into my work. The male P.E.teacher that had been there since my hiring had retired and the physical education program had transitioned well to being co-ed. I so enjoyed teaching the boys and the girls together. The curriculum was now life skills based. Instead of throwing a round ball through a round hoop, playing team sports or attempting to do gymnastics, students learned how to play tennis, golf, volleyball, badminton, square dance, snowshoe, ping pong, pickleball and cross country ski, things they could do in their life alone or with others.

I worked to get my Curriculum Coordinator certification as well as being one of sixty people in Maine to become certified in Adaptive P.E.; designing and implementing P.E type programs for children and adults with physical and or mental challenges. It was to be some of the most rewarding work I did. I learned from those amazing people what trust was all about. Being tethered to a blind person while downhill skiing was all about trust. Carrying a young man with cerebral palsy into a pool and having him say to me, with his face inches away from my own, "Coach, you are not going to let me drown, are you?" was trust. I would tell those students that they were going to fall head first in the snow, that they would go underwater and come up coughing; they knew what to expect and I would be doing it all right along with them. Truth and laughter, I learned, are the bedrock of trust. That same year I was named the State Coordinator for Girls and Women in Sports and had many opportunities to continue assisting and advocating for equality. My committee work both at the local and State level in the fields of health and wellness was ongoing. I was involved with work being done statewide identifying young women and young men dealing with eating disorders.

The high school health teacher and I were given the task of designing a system wide HIV/AIDS awareness curriculum that would be age appropriate for each grade level. The early eighties was consumed with the spread of the disease and it could not be approached without speaking openly about gay people or drug needle use. Having lost a couple friends and a few acquaintances to the ravages of the illness I knew the importance of educating our students about the disease and making them aware that it could kill them. It was the tool that enabled our school community to edge its way into the broader world of life outside of a small rural Maine town. It was not completed or implemented without tensions and lengthy discussions. Upon completion it was adopted as part of our health curriculum in the school system and we were asked to present it at a forum held in central Maine to school educators. It had not been easy or comfortable work. I continued coaching and being a student advocate. In 1992 I was honored as the State of Maine Physical Education Teacher of the Year. I was humbled, but living my duplicitous life had continued and it was taking a toll.

I was paying a mental fee living this way. I was trying to figure out not only who I was but what I was about. The pressure of trying to socially conform to what everyone in the world was telling me I should be, trying to get over the Catholic guilt and trying to accept myself was eating at me as surely as a black crow feasting on road kill. It was exhausting and stressful. There were times I thought I would become just a sliced fissure of who I knew myself to be. I decided I could no longer continue living in that pressure cooker. In the late 1980's I came out to myself. The rapture of calm that engulfed me was almost immediate. The person looking back from the mirror was indeed gay; I was women identified. I had been in a loving relationship, as loving a relationship could be for me or so I thought.

By the end of the 1980's I had completed my Masters Degree work in School Administration. I had finished my curriculum work and had integrated the life skills physical education program. I was ready to give up many years of coaching. I was ready and wanting new challenges. Spring arrived and I began to actively network and interview for middle School or high school principal's positions for the following school year, both in and out of state. I was on the "shortlist" for a position in Maine and one in Florida when I was contacted by my school's new superintendent who asked me if I would consider taking the position of principal at our local junior high. I said I would consider it but would like to meet with the School Board before I made a decision. I needed a clear idea of what their expectation was of me. The junior high was in the midst of philosophically transitioning to a middle school as well as being in desperate need of a new physical school building.

I had been in the school district for years; had taught and mentored hundreds of young ladies and young men, been in the public eye, had been active in my church, served on local and statewide committees and was the recreation director for a number of years. I knew many people and they knew me.

WINTER 1982

I was 32 years old when I found out that my Mom was really my aunt and my aunt was really my biological mother. My brother and sister were really my cousins. My cousin was my half sister and I had no idea who my biological father was.

Mom was preparing to have heart by-pass surgery. One evening she called me and asked if I could come to dinner the next night because she had something she wanted to tell me. This was so unlike my Mom. I knew she was going to have the surgery but perhaps her condition was more critical than I already knew. I began to imagine all sorts of things.

I arrived at her apartment the next day, knocked and walked in, and saw Mom in the kitchen. When she turned to greet me, I saw fear in her eyes. She was frightened. I gave her hugs and held her and said "What's wrong Mom, just tell me." She took my hands and led us to the couch where we sat very close. I put my arm around her back and told her I loved her. She took a deep breath and with tearing eyes she looked up at me and said "Sweetheart, you did not grow under my heart, but you sure grew in it." A silent pause followed, quiet enough to hear the frost growing on her glass patio door. I searched her aging face and said "Where did I come from?" Mom looked down at our entwined hands. I was holding my breath. Not a word was spoken for what seemed like a long time. Mom raised her head and just looked at me. She said not a word, only looked with those frightened eyes. I blurted out "Aunt Ida! I have her chin and nose!" Mom nodded her head in affirmation.

I was so worried about Mom's feelings that I didn't process my own, for a long time; years in fact. We held each other. I told her she would always be my Mom and that I would always love her dearly, no matter what. Ribbons of tears cascaded down our faces as we continued to embrace. With tissues spent, noses blown and breaths taken we began to talk. The first thing I exclaimed was "At least my Mémère was still my Mémère!"

"Why now, I asked?" Mom told me that Dan had been urging her to tell me the truth for a long time. He feared if anything happened to her I would never believe him or anyone else. She told me that both Lucy and Dan were told about my adoption back when they had graduated from high school.

Mom told me that no one knew that Ida was even pregnant, not even Mémère. I was born in Mémère's house, on "The Hill" in Augusta on a Sunday morning while Mémère was at church. One of the brothers, Sal, happened to be at Mémère's at that time. I was told he went to find the doctor and that the doctor came to the house and Ida and the baby were taken to the hospital. Sal then immediately went to get Mom. She told me that Sal drove her to the hospital.

Mom said that when she arrived at the hospital, Ida was distraught. She was praying a Novena on her rosary. She told Mom she did not know what she was going to do. I was just barely five pounds, born a couple of months earlier than expected. Mom knew that Ida had all she could handle with one child and Mémère had already birthed seventeen children and raised fourteen; she was worn out. Mom told me she went to see the baby in the nursery. A tiny little blond-haired, blue-eyed bundle is how she described me. Mom said she fell in love with me at first sight. When Dad got home from work that evening she told him about Ida and the beautiful little baby girl. Being a man of few words Dad said nothing, he just listened. Mom's story went on to say that the next morning Dad looked at Mom and said "Let's go see that little baby." They went to the nursery and then talked. They went to see Ida and told her they would take the baby. Ida was beyond thankful and relieved; she told them her prayers had been answered. She also told them that she would never, in any way, interfere with them raising me.

I had been told growing up that all three of us kids had been born by caesarean section because Mom's hips were too narrow to have natural childbirth. I was also told growing up, that Mom had wanted more children but could not have them.

Mom went into her bedroom, returned with an envelope and handed it to me. It was from the Maine Department of Health and Human Services; it was my adoption paperwork that my brother Dan held on to for safe-keeping for many years. I needed time to just quietly process this information. Neither one of us ate much dinner. I asked Mom if she was okay; a very familiar smile appeared and I knew she would be alright. I told her that I would call her the next day and proceeded to leave for a slow quiet solitary drive back home. I didn't know what being in shock was, but all of a sudden nothing seemed okay. The secrets, the lies, the silence; my head and my heart had been thrown into a swirling vortex of chaos. I didn't know how or where to even begin deciphering all this new information, never mind feeling anything about it.

I had trouble staying focused teaching my classes the next day and was relieved when the day was over and it was Friday. I called Mom when I got home; told her I loved her, asked if she was alright and then asked her to set up a meeting with herself, Aunt Ida and me. A short time later Mom called me back to ask if I could come to her apartment the next day, around four o'clock. Ida would be there. I thanked her and said "I'll see you soon; I love you Mom." Sleep and rest were fleeting things that night.

BETTY ANN THURSTON

I walked into Mom's apartment that sunny cold Saturday afternoon and there sat Aunt Ida, her friend Arnold, Mom and her friend Roy. They were sipping a "smile" and were warm and welcoming. I could only imagine what they may have been talking about before my arrival. I looked at Aunt Ida and said "Thanks for coming, I do have some questions for you." We proceeded to walk into Mom's bedroom. Aunt Ida sat in the chair and I on the corner of Mom's bed. I looked at her and said "What happened?" So began Ida's story and this is what she told me.

She said that she was angry that her husband Sam did not return to her after serving in the service in Europe during WWII. She told me that she knew he was in the States and what he was doing and that "she decided to do the same thing." I asked her who was my biological father and she replied with "It was a one night stand; his name was Lawrence Collins, he lived somewhere on upper Bridge Street. He was tall, blonde and blue eyed." She said "he did not know about me being pregnant; I never saw him again after that night."

Ida went on telling me that no one knew she was pregnant except for her brother Sal. She thought she had more time and said the plan with Sal had been that the following week he was going to take her to the train station where she would travel to St. Andre's Home for Unwed Mothers in southern Maine and leave the baby there for adoption. She went on to tell me how relieved and thankful she was when Mom and Dad agreed to take the baby. She named the child Betty Ann after her best friend. She was not planning on having to name that child. There were no tears on my face at this time but slow quiet tears filled the corners of her eyes. I sat quietly in the bedroom, rubbing the bed spread with the palm of my hand and touching Mom's rosary that always sat next to her bed pillow. I was numb; questions never came to me at that time. I did look at her and I said "thank you, that all must have been very hard, particularly since you were always around my life." Ida went on to say that Doreen was told about my adoption when she was in high school. I told Ida how much I loved my family and that Mom would always be my Mom. I then said "I am very thankful that you never caught a ride on that train." We both laughed with nervous energy and walked back into the livingroom to join the others. I was ready to sip a "smile" too.

As the weeks, months and years passed I had the opportunity to share Ida's story with some of Mom's sisters. Mom, her sisters and Celia would all get together for a weekend in the summer that they referred to as "The Sisters Weekend", a yearly tradition. Celia had no sisters and was like family so she was included. Since I was not married, had no children of my own and had some time available, they felt free to request me to be their designated driver and bar tender. I got to spend a little time with each of them individually and would ask questions about what or if they knew anything about my adoption. The general feeling was that yes, they were aware of it, but it was never mentioned or spoken about at all, with anyone. They never shared it with their children, my cousins. All agreed that I was fortunate to be in Mom and Dad's family. I told them

"absolutely!" Those conversations never left me feeling like the truth had been completely unveiled. I had a clear sense that neither the aunts nor Mom could, or that they would, confirm all the information as true. I had been told stories from Ida and stories from Mom and doubt had laid it's thick smothering blanket over my thoughts.

I asked Mom how Betty Ann got changed to Jacqueline Marie. She told me that my sister Lucy had a friend who had a baby sister named Jacqueline and that Lucy would tell Mom that she wanted a baby Jacqueline, too. I was brought home from the hospital that February in 1950 and introduced to my three year old sister and six year old brother as baby Jacqueline. My name change and adoption were not officially completed until months later.

I wanted to trust the information told to me. I wanted to believe it was the truth. I wanted to trust the people telling me these stories. I didn't trust. I had been told untruths for so long; so many stories. I didn't know who or what to believe. I felt like the ground was giving way and the tent poles were coming down.

I found the secrecy of my adoption, never being spoken of or referred to in the world of my large family for over thirty years beyond my comprehension. With all the gatherings, all the drinking, it never came out. I found it difficult to believe. As time went on I would learn why it was kept silent.

Mom and I would speak of my adoption again. It was at one of these times that Mom told me she believed that my Dad was my biological father. I can't say that I was shocked to think that but my heart and soul were ruptured with hearing my Mom say that she felt her husband had slept with her sister. I asked Mom if she had ever confronted Ida about this. She said she had not, not yet.

Ida and Arnold had been dating for twenty years off and on. They each had their own homes and in 1974 they finally got married and moved into a new home. I would continue to see them; they remained in my life but there was no more talking about my adoption. There was nothing more to say. Ida was in her eighties when she had her first stroke. She would labor to walk and talk and needed assistance. Arnold kept her at home, taking very good care of her every need until another stroke left him with no choice but to place her in a care facility where he would faithfully visit her every day. I visited her a few times, would call her often to tell her thank you and that I loved her for what she did for me. Ida passed in 2008. I had been privileged to write and deliver eulogies for a few of my aunts, uncles and friends. Arnold asked me to do the same for Ida. He also asked me to sit beside him during the funeral and if I would carry Ida's urn out of the church. I agreed. I was told by Arnold that my half sister, Doreen, had not treated her mother very well. He said that Doreen never spent much time with Ida and that he would have nothing to do with her or her husband because of a legal matter that had occurred among the four of them over the purchase of Ida and Arnold's condo. I asked if he thought they would come to her funeral. His reply was "I don't know and I don't care." The day of the funeral arrived and we walked out of Arnold's home and saw Doreen and her husband pulling up. I greeted them and gave them a hug; it had been years since I had seen them. Arnold glared at them, not a word spoken, and got into the car. I saw the bad blood first hand.

The church was full of long time friends and of course family members. Ida and Arnold had lived and worked in the area for decades. The priest was Arnold's nephew. When it was time for the eulogy he, the priest, introduced me as "Ida's special niece." I knew what I had written to deliver that day, and it was not written from a niece but from a daughter. I publicly thanked Arnold for taking such good care of our mother. I could see people looking at each other trying to figure out what I had just stated. I perused the congregation, my eyes went directly to my Mom; I wanted her to know it was okay. She would always be referred to as "my Mom", Ida as "my mother." Folks were shifting in their pews, glances traveled around; they had caught it. After the ceremony Arnold and I stood in the entrance to the church greeting people, thanking them for coming. He introduced me to all of their friends with "this is Ida's daughter, Jackie." "Oh you look like your mother." I would hear that a few more times in my life. My half sister Doreen stood beside me for a few moments. I thanked her for coming. That day is the last time I saw or heard a word from her.

GROWING APART

In the early 90's I had come out to my brother and sister. They were not shocked; they just wanted me to be happy. They were very loving and supportive. I told them that I would tell Mom when I was ready. They agreed it was my story to tell. My sister Lucy broke that trust. She told Mom that I was gay. I was deeply hurt. I had trusted Lucy. Since I did not have much trust or believe in lots of things in my life at that time, that rubbed salt into the wound. I told Lucy I was disappointed in her and that it was not her place to say anything to Mom. I went ahead and made plans to sit with Mom and tell her that I was gay. I told Mom I had always been gay, that it was nothing that I chose to be, I was born that way. I told her of the ongoing fight I had waged with myself trying not to be gay. I will forever remember my Mom's response to me. She looked up and said "Well, we don't ever have to talk about this again." I just looked at her. I knew she was disappointed in me. I never wanted to disappoint my Mom, ever. My insides were shivering as if I had taken a polar plunge. We never spoke of my being gay again. I had learned that Mom had a way of dealing with or should I say, not dealing with unpleasant or difficult things. They just would never be spoken about; therefore they didn't exist.

I certainly did not flaunt being gay, but I was not a girly girl. I never had been and surely was not going to try to be one now. I was beginning to see my authentic self. I was a good person who was very aware of other people's feelings but could not find or express my own. My personal life was on shaky ground at this time but what I knew for sure was that I still took good care of my partner and supported her in every way I could. I tried to get her to aspire to take courses at a local college; I offered to pay for her education but she had some low self esteem issues and was happy just having a job. It was okay with me. I had done my share of blue collar work and was proud of the skills I learned. What became an obstacle for me in our relationship over the years was her "settling" for things. She was not one to do any real self-examining and seemed to blame her mother for many things. We clearly had grown into two different people. My world was expanding. I had a growing number of colleagues statewide; I was out many evenings at meetings and events. My horizons were changing as sure as the sunrise and sunset hues; hers were not. Still I loved her the only way I knew for many years.

AUGUST 1993

My decision to take the principalship in the same community that I had been teaching and coaching in for so many years was made. The School Board's expectations were clear; transition a junior high school into a middle school philosophically and get a referendum passed (it had failed twice before) in the community so that a new middle school facility would be built. I knew I would have supporters and opponents. The majority of the junior high staff were in favor of the changes that would be coming but a few wanted things to remain the way they always had been. I was upfront and direct with them. I told them I did not like surprises and that I would support them in their work as long as they were truthful with me. If they chose to be less than truthful then I would not stand behind them. This did not settle well with a few staff members. Some were used to being coddled and in my opinion a couple of teachers had no business being in a classroom because I wasn't sure they even liked kids. Those folks did not see me as an advocate for them. I told those teachers in private conversations that I was not there to advocate for them but to advocate for all the children who sat in their classrooms day after day look-ing at them. I listened to kids and believed in them; not to say that I didn't know a story when a child would spin one for me. Sending children out of the classroom to the office because they were noncompliant, noisy, or because they were chewing gum was senseless. If they were belligerent, had a weapon or were out of control that was a different matter. That would be taken care of. Students that were sent to the office for some minor thing would be asked, by me, "What's the problem?" The response I would get most of the time would be "I don't know." I would reply with "Well, if you did know, what would it be" and most of the time they would come back with "He doesn't like me" or "She isn't fair." I would tell those staff members that they would have to find a way to work with that child because that student would be coming back to their classroom. Again, those few staff members became opponents of me and my decisions. I always wondered if it was my decisions they did not agree with or was it because of who I was, a gay woman.

Shortly after starting my work in this new position I knew I would have to be frank and truthful and talk with the superintendent about being gay. I wanted to be truthful. I had been threatened before by someone about making it public that I was gay and I refused to allow myself to ever have to deal with the threat of being blackmailed again. I knew my boss was a practicing Baptist and that's all I knew about him. I asked to meet with him. With my stomach tied as tightly as athletic tape around an ankle and with knees shaking I sat in his office. He looked at me and said "What's up" and my response was this. "I want to help you and or any Board member with the language you could use when you are confronted with "Do you know that you have a queer or a faggot up there running that school and yes, you will be confronted with this." I had his undivided attention.

I went on to tell him that I was gay and had a partner of some twenty years and the reason I was coming out to him was because I did not want to be in a position to be blackmailed. I proceeded to say that when he would be confronted with this topic he could say " Her orientation has nothing to do with her work. She is fair, doing a good job and that is all that matters." He shook his head in approval and told me he would speak individually with Board members should it be necessary. I told him that the next day I would be saying the same thing to the junior high staff. He thanked me for coming to speak with him.

The following day was a scheduled teachers' meeting. As the meeting came to a close, I said "This meeting is officially over but I have something that I would like to say to you should you choose to stay; it is optional." No one left the room. Again, stomach churning like a sea in a storm, I told them that yes, I was gay and yes I know that some of their students had asked them if I was gay.

I relayed once more the same words I had said to my boss and further stated that if they were at all uncomfortable talking to their students when they were approached about this subject they could always send them to me and I would answer their questions. Whenever a young student did ask me if I was gay I would respond with "What does that word mean to you?" Their replies were about the same; "It means you like girls." I would shake my head and say "Yes, I like girls and I like boys." They had their answer and went on their way.

The times in my life when I had been battered with slurs, spit at and had objects thrown at me would make me emotional. Those personal attacks are meant to hurt and do so to this day. It has nothing to do with having a soft heart as I have been told before. Any human would find those things hurtful. There were times in my position as principal when I would meet with parents of students who were not in favor philosophically with a middle school. They were clearly vocal about curriculum changes or, heaven forbid, any interscholastic changes. They were not in favor of any sort of diversity program that our guidance director was implementing. I was once asked by a Board member what I meant by "diversity." I explained that people who did not look the same as they did or dressed differently than they did, or spoke a different language or believed in a different religion was what diversity training was about. It didn't mean people who were different were bad, it meant they were just different. Middle school students are all about fairness and equality and they wanted to take action whenever they thought things or people were not treated fairly. That is just where a middle school age student is developmentally. I knew there was nothing I could say to folks who confronted me about these issues. I have to say that, at times, these challenges felt personal and the hurt would always be close by.

Progress continued in all areas of the transitioning of our school but not without some difficulties. The referendum passed. My taking a loaf of bread and quart of milk around to every senior citizen gathering for an entire year I believe helped to make the difference. I was told that the reason the referendum had failed on two previous occasions was because the senior citizens did not want their taxes going up. Most of those seniors knew me; I had taught and coached their children and grandchildren. I presented to them that the financial burden on them for a new middle school would amount to raising their taxes just about as much as a monthly quart of milk or loaf of bread. Three years later we had our new beautiful school but not without exhausting work.

1995

I had met principals around the State who made their living traveling around getting new schools built and staged. It was a full time job. I had no assistant principal and there were many times I could not be in the building during the school day. (meetings with State approval boards, architects' meetings, merchandise supply people, site visits and on and on it would go). I would have to find a teacher or a specialist to stand in for me in my absence. Thankfully I had two excellent administrative assistants who kept the day-to-day school life in the office somewhat normal. Returning to the office at the end of a long day would mean lists and copious notes of business to be taken care of. It made for late nights and early mornings. It is always important for the climate of a school that the principal be seen and heard daily for both students and staff. I was close to drowning, just trying to keep my head above water and had to use triage as a way to function. It was beyond exhausting. I was responsible for what seemed like everything and had little control of anything. It is not a good place to be. My time was completely taken up with getting this new building up and supplied. Taking care of daily student discipline, checking to see how the new math curriculum was faring, doing teacher observations and evaluations, preparing budgets, working on bus issues, understanding low test scores, finding money for every school need, approving or declining field trips and making sure the soda machine in the teachers' lounge was filled were just some of the duties. The minutiae of daily details was stifling. It was not possible to do it all and do it well. Some of my staff understood this; others did not.

I would usually be at my office a couple hours before the first busses rolled in. One morning upon my arrival I saw graffiti sprayed over the walkway into the building, "QUEER." It was carefully placed for all to see. No one mentioned that graffiti to me but I knew some students and teachers were having conversations about it. It was removed that same day.

As the pressure to get work completed with set timelines increased I knew I needed some assistance and asked for it. The superintendent knew I was in an impossible situation and gave me permission to ask a couple of teachers to step up to take over some things that they could do; they would be compensated. This helped some. I needed tools to cope and withstand the barrage of work. So began my journey into the world of professional counseling and therapy. I was not a trusting person but I was trusted. I had learned how to disregard and not feel hurtful things at an early age and had not recognized that I had acquired those skills. Finding out about my adoption late in life brought a whole new slant on who I was or who I thought I was. A huge rug had been pulled out from beneath me and I was determined to bounce and not break. The silence, secrets and untruths told to me in my life were in the process of unfolding much like a mainsail in the wind. I did not know who to trust or who to believe. I had learned to place secrets, lies and silence within me, like an ice cube in a freezer; they morphed early on into pain and fear. I was not capable of expressing and knowing joy, peace, happiness or calm. I confused care, compassion and empathy with love. After months of tedious difficult work in the arena of therapy, the slow melting of those stacked ice cubes within began.

I will always remember the session that awakened the memory of the monster who lived in the brown and yellow two-story apartment building on the south side of the city. Uncontrollable guttural sobs racked my body as my memory woke. I thought I was shriveling like styrofoam meeting a flame. My mind and body reliving flashes of the scenes in that upstairs shed were at war with themselves. Until that very moment I had not a fleeting thought of being molested by Muller. As I sat with my counselor rewinding the scenes of my five year old self a new reality of understanding was born. I got it. I knew why I did not embrace our American flag or seeing all those little red white and blue flags stuck in planters, yards and mailboxes around the 4th of July made me uneasy. A silent ride home left me with fearful thoughts of two other little girls who lived in that brown and yellow two-story apartment building on the south side of the city. I knew why I had trust issues and why I always tried to do what I was told. I wanted to be a good girl. The vivid memory of being in the first grade when the nun told us that we should give up our two cent milk money, to not be selfish, and put it in a box in the front of the room so that the class could buy a pagan baby from some mission on the other side of the world ran through my brain like a commercial on a television. No one dared not give up their milk. No one wanted to be selfish. What an absolute con all that was! Trust was supposed to be learned from the people that raised you; if you could not believe and hold what they told you as true then where would trust be learned? The skill of questioning, to ask and not always accept "because I said so" or to dare to drink your milk instead of buying a pagan baby and not feel guilt was going to take time, a longer time than any cast covering a broken limb. It was going to take me time to heal.

It was about this time that I had written and sent a letter to the Board enumerating some of the philosophical differences of junior high programs vs. middle school programs. I was hoping to be able to present a case to them for some budgeted money to hire a person to run some middle school intramural programs. We were going to have our usually scheduled Board meeting and I wanted them to have the letter before the meeting. I had informed the super-intendent that I had sent a letter and told him what it was about. I thought my letter was clear but one Board member took it upon herself to show the letter to a couple selected parents and they decided that it sounded like I wanted to end the interscholastic sports programs. I, along with one of my staff members, was sitting in the Board meeting to answer some end of year eighth grade activity questions when four or five parents came into the meeting waving a copy of the letter. They were demanding to know what it was about. My superintendent was another person who did not like surprises. Since it was not on the agenda they were told that there would be a meeting the following week to discuss the issue. I looked at my staff member and whispered "We are going to need help."

A week I would like to forget ensued. The middle school staff was upset; they always felt that they were the red-headed step children in the district and that they had to conform to the wishes of what the high school thought they should be. They felt like they had spent too much time having to justify the decisions that were made. The staff rallied and asked parents who were supporters of them and their school to come be present at the scheduled and publicised meeting. Everyone was on high alert, particularly me. Almost the entire middle school staff showed up to the meeting. Many members of the community, parents, former students, and other teachers from the district were in attendance. The meeting was called to order by the Chairman of the Board and people were allowed to speak one at a time. I had prepared my comments ahead of time and was ready to tell the audience how much I valued sports and competition and the lessons and social skills that athletics offered to those who got to play them. I had spent my life teaching and coaching sports. Parents were aware that middle school students who were successful and had better skills had many community and state wide opportunities to play and compete in their sports. I had planned to say that those students who had special needs also had community wide programs that provided them with opportunities to play and compete; both ends of the student spectrum were covered but nothing existed for the kids in the middle of that spectrum which accounted for most of our students. An intramural program would fill their need to have an opportunity to play and compete against each other therefore having an opportunity to earn and learn confidence and success. This was what I planned to say. But by the time people voiced their fear of losing a sport or sports for their talented child, by the time the middle school philosophy of diversity and acceptance was questioned, by the time the Board member who gave the letter from me to a few vocal parents had been confronted with "Why did you do that?" and by the time a parent stood up, looked at me and said "How can she make decisions for our children when she has never been a mother" my emotional self was spent. The room became still. All eyes were on me. The rapid fire of that parent's words was a personal assault that was intended to hurt and harm. It critically wounded me. The Chairman of the Board looked at me and said "Would you like to say something?" I could not speak. I was pulverized by such a display of ignorance. This was personal. I tried to speak out, my voice was silent. I could not talk; I could not use the voice that I had used so often and openly for the good of others to defend myself. The Board assured those in attendance that the middle school was not going to lose their sports programs and the meeting was adjourned. The Board member who had given out her letter resigned under the pressure and intramurals were not funded for the middle school that year.

OCTOBER 1997

We, my partner and I, had made friends with a circle of lesbian women, consisting of former students, students' parents, professional colleagues, and new folks we had never met. It was empowering and comforting to be with other lesbians, to know you were not alone. Shared stories, both good and bad tightened our circle. I always looked forward to times spent with these women. It was the first time we could be open and ourselves with others. My partner did not feel the same way. She began saying things to me like "I know someone is going to steal you away from me." I would tell her I would not be stolen but told myself I could choose to leave. Some of the partners in our circle had decided to have commitment ceremonies because gay people were not allowed to marry at that time and it was a way to openly celebrate their union with family and friends. My partner thought we should follow suit and do the same. I believe she felt if we did have a ceremony that would take care of her insecurity about me "being stolen." I was not in favor of doing this, not at first. But, like so many times in our life together she would continue to keep bringing it up and over time, I would usually acquiesce. We began having conversations about a possible ceremony. She was not "out" to her family and did not ever appear to have the desire or ability to talk with any of them about us. I told her that I would want all of my family there, if we did it. I asked her who she would want to have at a ceremony. She said we had most of the same friends, knew my entire family and left it at that. She never came forward with a list of any kind. She continued talking about having a ceremony until I finally said okay, but if we are going to do this I want it to be done well and that there would be a strict budget to which we would have to stick. And so it began, the planning of our ceremony. In the process of all this arranging, I, for the very first time in my life, had met a woman who actually stirred my heart and touched my soul. It was a powerful smack; like a baseball leaving the bat headed for the fences. She was also in a long term relationship and the four of us became friends.

The day of our ceremony arrived. I was in a bedroom dressing for the event when Mom came in. She looked at me and said "I just want you to be happy." I replied with "I think this is as good as it gets for us." The days coming up to the celebration were difficult for me. Therapy had just begun turning the key to long held secrets and giving me permission to feel. Counseling had shown me that I had become selfless over the years. I took care of others' feelings at my own expense. As the day arrived I felt more sad than happy. In the past I knew that when it came to difficult things I would do the "right" thing and would generally speak up. I did not stop the ceremony, a regret I carry to this day.

As time went on I became more and more distant from my partner. I had made up my mind that I was going to leave her. Staying in the relationship would have been yet another selfless illustration; it was time for me to be selfish and look out for myself. It was not about what others would think about me; it was how I would think about myself. Ending that relationship was the second most difficult thing I ever did and it turned out to be the absolute best thing I ever did for myself. Divorce between heterosexuals who have been together for a couple decades is difficult enough but there are support systems for them. The parting of a long term gay relationship had no systems in place. It was a very lonely time.

LOSSES

It was a bitterly cold frosty January morning in 1996, the kind of cold that made the snow squeak when you walked on it; when your nostrils would all but freeze your nose hairs. I was laying my hands on the old silver radiator in my office when my phone rang. I picked it up and listened as a high school colleague told me that my good friend Peter, who taught at the high school for many years, had passed that morning from a heart attack as he was getting ready to come to school. The loss was unexpected; my sorrow was palpable. I went to the high school that morning to be with colleagues, to hug, to cry. The school was sad. He would be greatly missed by both students and staff.

Our new school was deeply under construction. We had little input to the style and layout of the new building; the site plan determined what it would be. Teachers had given me their wish lists of wants for their individual teaching spaces but it was indeed just that, a wish list. But a couple teachers thought they would get their list filled. It didn't happen. The superintendent told me that he would take care of the financial end of things and that I was to create invoices for every item we needed and how many of each of those items we needed. Teacher desks, classroom storage, chairs, phones, computers, tables, student desks, chairs, cafeteria tables, chairs, library stacks, library tables, chairs, office desks, photocopiers, conference room tables, chairs, televisions, wastebaskets, white boards, science lab tables, integrated learning project tables, benches, stoves, refrigerators, wastebaskets, teachers lounge seating and on it went. It was a daunting task. I was very thankful that one of my teachers volunteered to assist me in counting the number of how many of what was needed. I submitted the stack of invoices to my boss, on time. The end of that school year was drawing to a close and I had other pressing issues to deal with, professionally and personally.

We would finally be in our new school when Fall arrived and a new school year resumed. The junior high had housed grades six through eight but the new middle school would be housing grades five through eight due to the elementary school's growing student population. To help those fourth graders who would be leaving their familiar elementary school and would be becoming fifth grade students in the new middle school, it was decided that we would have them come in small groups, for a tour of their new school that was still under construction. As I was standing at the front door greeting these little people as they walked into the building I heard, "Never mind being gay, look how tall she is." This came from a young boy as he was approaching me. A smile stretched like a soft rubber band across my face. The innocence of youth was keenly displayed; it gave credence to just how soft a child's heart could be.

Most of that summer was spent physically moving into the new building. Students, staff and the community were excited. Teachers had space, no more portable classrooms, no more using old broom closets for one-on-one sessions, no more walking outside to go to an old cafeteria in an adjacent building. The new cafeteria was the last to be completed; it was not ready when school opened so the large multipurpose area in the new building was used as a temporary feeding station. By the end of October construction was completed. A dedication ceremony and open house was held for the community in early November. Students gave tours, answered questions and their school pride shined. Our endless hours of work were acknowledged. The superintendent and I were given plaques expressing gratitude. The open house was a great success and I now could cross off one huge task on the list.

I got a call at home one evening in early December. It was the Chairman of the Board. He told me that our superintendent was in the hospital; he had suffered a brain aneurysm, the prognosis was not good. In the early morning hours of a new December day he passed. My work world was on tilt. I called an emergency staff meeting that morning before school began and told the staff what had happened. I told them we had lost a huge supporter. I knew the middle school had lost its biggest advocate and that things had to carry on but I could not imagine how. Not only had I lost a boss, I lost a friend. We had spent many many hours together getting this new school built, up and running. We got to know each other and respected each other even when we disagreed. I felt like I was on a plane with no pilot. I had zero knowledge in how to fly a plane; I also had zero knowledge about the financial picture of paying for this new building. An anxiety inducing situation at the least. By mid- morning the Chairman of the Board called me and said "The Board and I would like you to be the interim superintendent." I was not prepared to hear that. I thought for sure the high school principal would be asked to fill in but my ongoing work with the new building made the difference, I believe. He told me to just "take care of things," to keep things running and that I would be compensated. I told him I was not comfortable stepping in and heard "You'll do just fine." I had no choice; it was a done deal. What I knew for sure was that I would be spending even less time in our new building for the foreseeable future and that this would not go over well with some of my staff. My goal was to get a superintendent for the district as soon as possible.

I did my best to spend time in my office and in the superintendent's office. Thankfully he had an excellent business manager who was well-versed in the financial end of all things school-related. Things came up everyday that needed attention in both places; again, without the help of very capable administrative assistants in each office, school business would have not continued smoothly.

At my frequent urging to the Board, a superintendent was hired by Easter. I could refocus on my work at the middle school. I had received my superintendent's certification and after my brief interim position I knew that job was too far removed from day-to-day experiences with kids for me.

Our programs and classes settled into a new rhythm. Glitches and adjustments were taken care of. Change was harder for some staff than for others. A couple teachers who struggled in the old school struggled in the new school. I was going to do my best to assist those tenured teachers whom I believed should not be in a classroom to see that it was time for them to perhaps seek other options. One or two did not agree with me but one or two did.

The new superintendent was eager to get the pulse of the school community. He knew I had been around a long time; in fact the high school principal called me "the local sage." It did not take him long to know who the players were. He would find out where the strengths and weaknesses sat in the individual schools; with staff and the local community. The two of us got to know each other. One day he asked me how I had been able to stay in that community for so many years. I replied with "Getting involved with kids, spending hours teaching and coaching and caring about programs just had a way of keeping me here." I also told him I thought my work was about completed.

In November 1998, on a crisp Fall afternoon, one of our longtime staff members, seemingly in good shape, who was a runner, had a seizure while he was jogging near school. He was diagnosed with a brain tumor that had metastasized from a melanoma that had been missed on his back. Our staff and students were saddened by the news. In March he passed. He would be greatly missed in our school. It was yet another jolt to our school community.

In April 1999, on a sunny Spring day the school district's overseer of transportation and maintenance passed from a heart attack. I had worked closely with him and had known him a long time as a local man with many family ties in the community. The blows to our school community kept mounting.

On an evening in November 1999, my home phone rang and it was the superintendent. He told me that our Chairman of the Board just died from a heart attack. I had all I could do to stay vertical.

Bob was well known in the community by kids and parents. He had a position working for the State of Maine in Augusta but lived locally and owned a roller rink where he was always present. Many of our students would be deeply saddened by this shocking news. In a three year span our small school system had lost five important figures. I don't believe I was alone in thinking who might be next.

I had experienced many losses in my life since my Mémère passed and knew that you never really forget the people that had literally stepped out of life, but you learn to adjust. A galactic hole had been carved into our school community that would take time to fill.

Life in the middle school continued to move ahead. New staff were hired, new programs implemented and thankfully for me, things were more manageable. On a Thursday morning in late October I had a visit from the superintendent. He came into my office, sat down and said "I have an offer available to you in appreciation for all of your work in this school system for so many years. It is completely up to you. Should you choose not to take it, you can stay here as long as you wish." I was intrigued. He was offering me the opportunity to resign my principal's position at the end of the school year with a very good financial package that had already been approved by the Board. If I turned it down I could remain as principal. The choice was mine. Unlike teachers, administrators had no unions or associations to do their bidding; we were on our own.

I had completed all the challenges and tasks that I was hired to meet. The Board's expectations of me had been met. My work was done and I felt good about it's completion. I was ready professionally and personally to move on. I took the offer and resigned but was asked to stay until the end of that school year.

On the last day of school that June I packed things into my car, gave my most sincere thanks and hugs to my two administrative assistants and walked out of the building. My time in the mill town on the banks of the Androscoggin River was over.

BIG SHIFT

I told my family that I had met a woman and had been dating her for a couple of months and that I was very happy. Being able to express my happiness was brand new to me. I also told them that I would be leaving my position at the end of the school year. Everyone was happy for me except Mom. She just could not understand why I would leave my administrative position; I was only fifty years old. I told her I would be okay financially, that I might even do some kind of fun job wherever we ended up living. I was ready for some completely new life experiences.

Mom and I had lunch together and I asked her if she had asked Ida about Dad. She looked at me and said she had and that Ida had absolutely denied it. I asked if she believed her; Mom shook her head "no." So I asked about Dad. I told Mom I remembered all the flirting that went on when they were drinking and asked if this is why she felt that Dad was my father. She told me about the time that he stayed out all night, did not come home until the morning, and she felt that he stayed with Ida. She did not share with me if they had fought about something but my experience with Mom never arguing with Dad made it hard for me to believe that this would have been why he stayed out all night. I asked her how this secret was kept quiet all those years, with all of her family being so close. She said that her sisters and brothers also believed that Dad was my father and it was just never spoken about. I believe her siblings remained silent out of respect for their sister, my Mom.

I told Mom that I had tried to find a birth certificate for Betty Ann Thurston but there was no such name on record at City Hall. "How could that be I asked?" In 1971 I needed a copy of my birth certificate to obtain my teaching credentials. I told Mom I was going to go to City Hall to get it during Christmas break, but Mom said she would get it for me. The next story Mom told me was that Dad knew a man who said he could take care of it so that no one would ever know about Betty Ann Thurston and that Mom and Dad would be listed on an official birth certificate as my parents. I was speechless. I looked at Mom and said, "That's against the law." Breaking the law to continue to hide a secret was nothing I ever thought would be in my Mom and Dad's realm of attempting. "That's how people disappeared," I said. I was beginning to think I did not know the people who raised me like I thought I did. I told Mom I needed time to think about all of this. Things were falling into place. Memories of the Punnett Square and why it didn't work out; my being given the option to go to a private Catholic high school while my brother and sister went to the public high school; Doreen's kids calling me Aunt Jackie; Ida being around my life and volunteering to do my laundry when I was at boarding school and Dad saying to me "Someday you'll know what we did for you" after seeing what I wrote on the bathroom window. It was making sense now.

One day I had business in Augusta and stopped in to say "Hi" to Mom. Her friend Celia, the neighbor lady who used to own the brown and yellow two-story apartment building, was there having lunch. They were in the middle of a conversation so I told them to continue; I had to use the restroom. As I came back towards them I heard "Muller was a dirty old man" from Celia. I stopped moving. Not another word was said. I began to ask myself if she and Mom knew and believed he was a dirty old man, why would they have asked me to bring him things? Why would this be kept so silent? I did not confront them. I just gave Mom hugs, asked if she needed anything and went on my way. I would always love my Mom but I began to think that she was not as perfect as my child's vision had seen her. I was disturbed by what I heard and my mind was taking me places I did not want to go.

I give thanks everyday for having found the love of my life. Relationships are made up of difficult avenues to negotiate and gay relationships are no different. There were no trails yet blazed for paths to parenthood for gays and lesbians in our younger days. I think we would have made good moms and would have wrapped our children in love.

For the first time in both our lives we could decide where to live not based on our work. After taking some months to travel and visit numerous places we chose an active, diverse and welcoming city in North Carolina to call home. My partner encouraged us to take the leap and begin to buy homes that we could either rent or fix up and flip. After her professional career as a College Dean she learned how to estimate, tear down, and do the physical work to rehab a property. While she tended to those tasks, I told myself I wanted to play with adults and wine. I was hired by the most visited winery in the country and had the opportunity to learn what it took to birth a fine bottle of wine. The adventure from a cloned vine to a finished bottle was one I was thrilled to be on. As many have said "Once a teacher, always a teacher". Soon I was the wine training coordinator for Biltmore Winery.

Mom passed in 2009. She had been living with Lucy and Will and loved being with them. Her dementia and weaknesses were growing; my sister and her husband needed to work. After much discussion with Dan and Lucy we knew we had to put Mom in a nursing home. It was the most difficult thing I have had to do. Telling Mom she would have to leave her daughter's home and go to some strange place was excruciating. Mom had no savings, only a small social security pension every month. Thankfully, she was only there a few months when she had a heart attack and passed. Mom was ninety-four years old. We were relieved for her; we knew she was unhappy and it broke our hearts. My siblings asked if I would give Mom's eulogy. There was a time I didn't think I could do it because I couldn't imagine my life without my Mom but things were different now; I was different.

It was a warm day in late June. We were back at our old family parish; it was all so familiar. Mom's grandchildren walked her casket down the aisle. My niece and nephew were adults now with children of their own. We followed her casket and took our places in the front pews. Mass began and the priest introduced me. I walked up to the lectern, turned and faced the kind people who had come to honor this woman. I saw some familiar faces that I had not seen in many years. One of those faces was Marilyn's little cousin Tess, now a woman close to my age. I paused. Mom had only two sisters still living; a dozen siblings had died over the years. The pews were not full; I smiled at seeing those empty seats because I knew there would have been a time when Mom would have made a comment about their emptiness.

Folks were gathered outside the church doors after the service. I wanted to speak to Tess who was there with her brother and his wife. I wanted to thank them for coming as her mother Celia, who had passed in 2003, and Mom were very good friends. I extended an invitation to them to come visit us in North Carolina. Tess responded immediately with "I would love to come for a visit some day; we will keep in touch." We did keep in touch over the years. We shared an uncle, the same uncle who teased and taunted the little girls. Tess's mother was a sister to that uncle. He was going to be celebrating his 95th birthday and family and friends were invited to attend his celebration in Atlanta. I had spent a lot of time with that uncle's family when I was a child. I wanted to go to this celebration and looked forward to seeing the cousins I grew up with. Tess told me that she and her brother and sister-in-law were planning on attending. I began to think about the possibility of having some alone time with her. I needed to ask her about the "dirty old man" that lived upstairs from them in that brown and yellow two story apartment building.

The time wasn't perfect but I did not know when I would see Tess again and it wasn't a conversation I wanted to have over the phone or by email. We were at my uncle's party; there was a time when it was just me, my partner and Tess. I took the step and told her that I was molested by Muller. Before our eyes we saw her literally wilt into the rocking chair behind her. Tears filled her eyes and pain swallowed her face. I knew, and now she knew about me. I told her this was not the time or place to discuss things but that I needed to tell her in person what happened to me because I didn't believe for a second that it only happened to me. She composed herself, we hugged and committed to talking soon. The next spring vacation from school where Tess was teaching, she flew down to visit us in North Carolina. So began the adult friendship with one of the little girls from the brown and yellow two-story apartment building.

Tess and her cousin Marilyn, my old friend, were in touch through the years. They have a very small family and always made an attempt to stay somewhat connected. Tess was able to give me Marilyn's contact information as we had left each other's lives as young adults. I sent her an email and so began our getting reacquainted. I was happy to have my old friend back.

Again, I wanted to speak with Marilyn about my being molested by Muller, but I wanted to do it in person. She was now living in north central Florida with a partner. My partner and I were going to be traveling to south Florida in late February and asked if she could meet us at a hotel where we would be staying on the way down. She was more than eager. I told her I would text her when we arrived at the hotel. I was just putting some things in our room when the phone in the room rang. It was the front desk telling me that there was a visitor in the lobby. I said I would be right down. I had no more than opened the door when this golden-haired, wide-eyed smiling face embraced me. It was wonderful to see each other after so many years. We sat out by the pool, shared some wine and told stories of old. I began to tell her my story and she said to me "How did he get to you?" The smiles and laughter were gone; the tears began. I told her about being asked to take some groceries up to him once in a while. She told me her painful past with Muller. She asked about Tess and I told her what I knew. Marilyn said "and that man would walk Tess to school many days." Three little girls, all shouldering the same pain because trusted adults didn't acknowledge the warning of "He's just a dirty old man," or didn't heed the small child shaking her head "no" and never asked why. Three little girls, all taught and raised the same way. You never questioned, you did what you were told and you respected your elders.

Many hours of reflection have taught me that my parents' era was formed by tight circles of family, along with the central positioning of the Catholic

Church and the indoctrinating of its decrees. The adversity of living through a world war and a depression, as well as the effects of their Franco-American migration to their self images left them with a preponderance for secrets, denials, and stoicism. Their worlds were small and local. They depended solely on themselves and their Catholic Church for guidance. No one taught silence any better than the Catholic Church. There was no internet, no hashtag movement nor fake news; they simply did not exist. It was not a part of their lives.

Child molestation was sadly nothing new and I couldn't help but wonder if some of their lives had not been cloaked in the same frozen silence that had been mine. I had told Mom what Muller had done to me. Her reply was that nervous chuckle and "I'm sorry."

Two years after Mom died, an aunt called me. She was the wife of one of Mom's deceased brothers. She was old, not well, had cancer and only a short time to live. She told me the reason she called was to say that everyone was gone now, and that she had lived with Ida during some of those early years; they had been friends. Ida never confirmed it to her, but she believed that Dad was my biological father. She had witnessed Dad flirting with other women, herself included, and thought it to be true. I thanked her for the call and said "It really does not matter to me anymore. The Dad who raised me will always be the Dad in my heart."

No one was left to ask, to talk to or to hear stories from. I believe Mom and Dad did what they thought was best to protect me. It was time to trust that decision.

Accepting that I had done nothing wrong to cause being molested, or adopted, or gay, or catholic took nearly a lifetime.

EPILOGUE

In June 2019 I got a Facebook message from one of my numerous cousins that said "It looks like you have another half- sister." This cousin had done a DNA test and a woman showed up as a relative. They contacted each other and shared some information. The woman was adopted in 1952 from St. Andre's Home for Unwed Mothers in southern Maine. The mother listed on her birth certificate was Ida Thurston from St. Quentin, New Brunswick.

I knew about DNA testing; Mom and Dad did not. I thought I would have to have some of Dad's DNA to confirm if in fact he was my biological father. After speaking with my new half-sister and my brother and sister, I decided to do a DNA test and asked my brother Dan,(really my cousin) to take it as well. If it came back and showed that he was my half-brother then we would know the truth; Dad and Ida would have slept together. He agreed to do the DNA test but then one Saturday afternoon I got a call from him telling me that he just could not take the test. It was like getting hit with a line drive to the gut. He told me he didn't trust where the DNA information might end up or how it might be used. I did not respect his decision; I thought it was extremely self-ish, not the brother I knew. I told him I had to get off the phone; I was very upset and he knew it. After a couple of torturous weeks he called to say he had changed his mind. He would take the DNA test. I had not asked him to change his mind. I told myself I wasn't going to ask him again. My sister Lucy was relieved that he had a change of heart and she was excited and hopeful that we would be real sisters, not cousins. No matter what, Dan and Lucy would always be siblings in my heart.

Weeks passed and the results came in. I did indeed have a new half-sister. Dan was still my cousin, not my half-brother and Lucy told me that she was sorry that she had believed Dad was my real father. The truth of DNA is final but the doubt that my Dad could have been unfaithful to my Mom will remain. That could be why he told Mom "Let's go see this little baby."

"The greatest gift we give to each other is the telling of the truth."

Maya Angelou

Thank you for reading my story. Reviews help others discover my book so please consider leaving an honest review on www.barnesandnoble.com/ review/ or any other review site you choose.